The All-American

MAN CLUB MEMBERSHIP MANUAL

KEEPERS OF THE ALL-AMERICAN MAN CARD

A Guide to Help Guys
GET THEIR SACKS BACK

Little Known Fact: There is no such thing as vagina envy.

By **TL Blake**

Published by Forrest F. Nelson

Copyright 2017 TL Blake and Forrest F. Nelson

Copyright © 2017

All rights reserved. No part of this publication may be reproduced, distributed or transmitted in any form or by any means, or stored in a database or retrieval system, without prior written consent of the Author.

PREFACE

Anonymous Gambler: There are three things in this man's world that run hot or cold. When they're hot, you gotta jump on 'em, ride 'em hard and fast. When they're cold, you gotta get off 'em, get far away, and leave 'em the hell alone! Those three things are: Cards, Dice, and Women!

Do you, like millions of other guys, wish you could:
Understand Women?
WE DO!
We know what women want, and we can give it to them,

If they behave.

If you are like most men, you have struggled for years trying to understand why women do what they do, why their behavior is so irrational, and how you can avoid the tribulations associated with any breach of protocol on your part, however unfathomable or unintentional. Well, you are not alone! Millions of men around the world share the same complaint: How to know what's going on in that pretty little head of theirs, and how to keep them happy. Most of all, men want to know WHAT WOMEN WANT!

Your struggle, our struggle and those of countless other men is the reason why we wrote the book and founded the All-American Man Club. This manual is a guide to help you achieve the freedom to become the man you were destined to be. In it you will find helpful phrases, questions and answers, lists of both approved actions and punishable behaviors, as well as a wealth of ideas for what to do when she tries to grab your mansack, metaphorically speaking. You will see how to either garner or lose valuable points on your All-American Man Card. There are sections dealing with relationships, and valuable All-American Man Club Principles. Of course, we will reveal women's Achilles Heel and the coveted secret to *What Women Want*.

You will learn how to have your pie and eat it too!

♂ Before we go any further, we need to make one thing perfectly clear: We're not misogynists, we don't hate women. Quite the contrary, we love women. We love the way they look; their supple curves and soft, silky skin. We love the way they smell, and the way they taste; as long as they follow rudimentary hygiene protocols, of course. Nobody likes too much cheese on the taco. We don't condemn their relentless pursuit of power, or their brazen use of feminine charms. They are simply doing what they do best. If anything, we respect their clever, if evil, use of their natural resources. You can't hate salmon for swimming upriver, it's what they do. Yes indeed, we do *so* love and admire women. In fact, of all the gifts that have been bestowed upon mankind throughout history, we like women the best.

We simply refuse to be manipulated, threatened, controlled or governed by them. Our motto is *Unicus Dominus Vir.* This is Latin, and for those of us unencumbered by classical education, Unicus means only one; Dominus means ruler, and Vir refers to man. Ergo, Only One Ruler. That ruler is MAN.

♂ Have you heard of Valarie Solanas, a radical feminist who

published the *SCUM Manifesto*, an anti-male game plan in 1967? In it she states that men have ruined the world, and calls for women to fix it. The acronym stands for the Society for Cutting Up Men, and the organization was dedicated to overthrowing society and eliminating the male sex! This is one example of why we need Members.

Imagine a world controlled by women. No, we mean openly, not the way it is now with women lurking in the shadows, secretly controlling men. What kind of world would that be? Mandatory chick-flicks and classes to teach us how to explore and connect with our feminine side? An end to Friday night poker, replaced by dusk-to-dawn cooking shows and shopping networks? And, dare we think it, an end to competitive sports? No more hockey, basketball, golf? No more…no, don't say it...we can't bear it...no more football?!! We can't go on, it's too painful. Changes must be made!

If you're ready to join us, to take that first step toward gender-based reapportionment of your social, personal, and relationship status, then follow us, join the club, learn and live the message contained herein!

In the process, not only will you achieve a new level of self-determination, a greater sense of self-worth and self-esteem; you will also get your sack back!

Do it now, before you lose your nerve. Join us, get the book, buy a T-shirt! Stop being so freaking frugal and spend some cash on yourself for a change!

♂♂♂

TABLE OF CONTENTS

Preface iii
Chapter One: An Act of Social Defiance 1
Chapter Two: Here's the Problem 6
Chapter Three: Femicomms and Entertainment 15
Chapter Four: Curses and Lists 20
Chapter Five: Aberrations 29
Chapter ~~Sex~~ Six: What Women Want 35
Chapter Seven: Threatening Situations 46
Chapter Eight: AAMC Guiding Principles 51
Chapter Nine: Useful Phrases 66
Chapter Ten: Places and Spaces 76
Chapter Eleven: Random Manly Thoughts 83
Chapter Twelve: Finding the Right Woman 93
Chapter Thirteen: They Are Just So Cute… 102
Chapter Fourteen: Penalties for Non-Masculine Behavior 109
Glossary 115
About the Authors: 119

♂ *There is an actual book out there that purports to be able to teach women how to make a man behave in 21 days or less using the secrets of professional dog trainers!*

Go ahead, be angry.

CHAPTER ONE:
AN ACT OF SOCIAL DEFIANCE

That's it! We have had enough! The time has come for all good men to walk, talk, and BE MEN! No more matching outfits, no more excursions to the mall for shopping on Sundays in the fall. No more men who aren't afraid to cry, and no more explorations of our feminine side! No more namby-pamby where do want to eat honey, I don't know, where do you want to eat? I don't know… No more derisive jokes referring to 3½ minutes or inches. And no more male facial hydration soaps, oils, or any other male beauty products. That's not manhood, it's servitude.

STOP FEMININE POWER!

We stand at the crossroads of our gender; will we face it standing erect with pride, or sniveling on our knees? If we are going to be men, we need some social reconstruction. We need to win back our testicles from the evil scourge known as *feminism*.

We need a revolution, nay, a counter-revolution!

We have unwittingly empowered women for decades. We accepted the changing roles of women in our society, albeit with some kicking and screaming. We reluctantly accepted the first females into what were essentially manly jobs because we didn't see them as a threat. We didn't even see them as women. Mostly they were stout little creatures of indiscriminate gender who wore Birkenstocks and Elvis hairdos.

We were begrudgingly "ok" with the inner strength of female television icons from Mary Tyler Moore' Mary, and Candace Bergen's Murphy Brown to Geena Davis' McKenzie Allen, and Tea Leoni as Madame Secretary. While not *everybody* loved him, even Ray's wussified and hopelessly whipped character was tolerated, if cynically dismissed, as comedy. In the real world, the USA has endured a few female Secretaries of State in recent decades. We nearly had a female President; THAT was a close call! But when an international cable news network aired a report of a woman underhandedly using dog-training techniques to alter the behavior of another woman's husband, we could stand no more! Women have gone too far.

The counter-revolution, like good beer, has been brewing for some time. The proliferation of male bashing has brought it to a head. No longer will we cower at the feet of women, afraid to utter a masculine thought lest it be mistaken for an act of piggish chauvinism. Men everywhere need to stand like men, straight, erect, strong, and much like a cold beer, with a good head.

Grab a mug and drink deep from the vat of revolution!

Before you read any further, check your package. Are your genitals on the outside? If they are still there, and you haven't surrendered them, you must know that you were born to become a MAN. Now let go of them, we have work to do.

Caution: if you are not prepared to join your brothers in this epic struggle to reclaim our natural birthright as the dominant gender on this planet, do not read this manual! Go exfoliate yourself!

For you, we suggest that you go to your significant other/wife/girlfriend/live-in/, heretofore referred to as her, she, or that woman, and ask her to loan you your testicles. You won't need them for long, just long enough to gather the courage you'll need to jump off a bridge, or lie on the tracks in front of an oncoming train, or finally tell her that if she doesn't want to look ridiculous in those hip-hugger jeans and tube top, she needs to lose fifty pounds. Any of those choices will result in you getting exactly what you deserve. On the other hand, if the thought of suddenly reclaiming your sack makes you feel especially ballsy, consider talking to an All-American Man Club Member. He can enlighten you, maybe even free you to become the man you were destined to be.

If you are ready to throw off the shackles of feminine domination, to stand defiantly against the cracking of the whip, and to boldly walk as though you do indeed have a set of hangers, then read on. Learn the truth, and join us as we take back what once was ours, our manhood!

We are men who have banded together to halt the onslaught of feminine power. Far too long has the natural balance of power swung in favor of the wily beguilers, we're going to change that. Fully confident in our ability to accomplish our mission of ending our enslavement, we are confident in our advantage. We know women.

We know their needs and desires. We know their strengths, and more importantly, we know their weaknesses. We know *why* they think the way they do.

For centuries men have been confused by women, and shared a common drive: To find out WHAT WOMEN WANT. Well, *we know*. We're here to share that elusive knowledge with you. If you are ready, we can show you. We are members of the All-American Man Club who proudly carry our All-American Man Card with as a symbol of our freedom from pussopression.

But for all those feminists worshipping at the Shrine of Steinem, relax. This manual is not intended to cast all women in a negative light (although when you get down to it, most women are pretty evil, you gotta admit…). Nor are we saying that women can't be whatever they want to be. If they want to be combat soldiers, go be combat soldiers; just don't be the weakest link in the chain. If they want to be homemakers, then go be homemakers; nothing wrong with either one. Whatever they want to be, they can go be it! Just leave men alone to be men. There is no reason that women can't fulfil their hearts' desires without taking away from men. We gave them a rib, what more do they want? Cheeezzz!

♂ In a world where Hall of Fame Pro Football player and former Head Coach "Iron" Mike Ditka is on TV pitching cures for Erectile Dysfunction, it is easy to see how women are gaining control. What vestiges of masculinity remain? We wonder if all those years of being around the finely tuned bodies of elite professional athletes in the showers caught up with him and took all the iron out of old "Iron" Mike. Be warned! The same can happen to you if you spend too much time around *the fridge*.

 ♂ How about those ancient builders? They didn't construct their sacred halls with wimpy blossoming flower petals, they built them with stiff solid shafts. They knew how to show off, and how to show the world who was who, and *why*. Here's a subtle reminder.

Now, we don't know what these look like to you, but to us, it's pretty obvious. The architecture reflects a time when men were bold enough to proclaim their rightful dominion; a time when men were not afraid to openly admire the natural beauty of nature, including women, and to celebrate the natural endowments with which each gender has been blessed.

We are not afraid!

Hey btw, remember that *SCUM* chick Valarie Solanas? We don't know if guys remember this or not, but she shot and tried to kill famed artist and self-avowed, near-male Andy Warhol. Really, Andy Warhol? Not exactly the manliest representation of the men the *SCUM* organization women wanted to cut up. Just sayin'.

We are still not afraid.

♂ ♂ ♂

> ♂ *A New York based female psychologist recently appeared on television and stated that men have very basic needs. She stated words to the effect that you just give them what they want and you can get them to do anything.*

CHAPTER TWO:
HERE'S THE PROBLEM

For countless eons on this planet, there was order. Early on our species struggled to gain a foothold in an incredibly dangerous and hostile environment. We busied ourselves with the everyday challenges of survival; procuring food, water, shelter, and what certainly must have been everyone's favorite, procreation. Sure, there were the obligatory, almost natural, minor skirmishes and outright wars occasionally, but for good reasons. We needed to protect what we had, and we needed to get whatever anyone else had that was better. Men were in charge!

Ah, those were heady times; when men made courageous decisions and women instinctively understood and accepted the natural order. There were no emotional discussions, no touchy-feely explorations of our feminine side. We knew what we wanted and we went out and took it! Think about it, ever seen a cave drawing depicting a female bitching out her man because his chunk of mastodon was smaller than the guy's in the cave next door? No. Why not? Because Old Bonk wouldn't have put up with Gronnika's crap!

Throughout recorded history, men continued to rule the species so thoroughly that one could describe this domination as pre-ordained. Whether you believe in religion or evolution, divine intention or just a crapshoot doesn't really matter. What does matter is that men were meant to rule. We were built for it, we fought for it, and we earned it. What's more, we deserve it!

However, as the adage goes, societies get exactly the type of government they deserve. If we are complacent and accept government by women, then we deserve to forfeit our sacks.

Do you, for a minute, think Attila the Hun ever allowed any of his wives to lie around the tent and whine, *"What about MY needs?"* Of course not. He was in command! He knew how to handle women, all men did. And what about good old King Henry the Eighth? He had a certain charismatic, if permanent, control over women. Probably set their movement back a couple of hundred years.

Everything went along just fine for centuries. We were all happy just to be alive. There were new worlds to be explored and conquered, new riches to be won, and new peoples to be subjugated and exploited. Men were out being men; women were at home, doing what women did. We didn't know what they were doing, exactly, but whatever it was, it kept them happy and, most importantly, quiet. We were all content in our roles, until they launched their diabolical plan. The plan was code named:

The Three Cons: Confuse, Control, Conquer

It probably began almost as soon as they realized they weren't in charge. Their distaste at being second citizens and placed just above sheep, coupled with their lust for power, sowed the seeds (maybe apple) of discontent. The countless passage of time under the control of men only frustrated them more and more until their discontent became venom, the malevolence of which we are only now beginning to understand.

Their movement grew quietly, subdued, passed in hushed whispers in small clandestine groups of women at watering holes, pot-bellied stoves, and heartland hearths. Oh, the depths to which they stooped! Then when the time was right, sometime during the last couple of centuries, The Plan was put in action.

First, they used cunning to get the right to vote. How was that accomplished, you ask? They withheld sex! Yes, there, we said it. We know how shocking that is, but imagine how utterly shocked and confused the poor men of that era must have been!

Never before had they experienced such unimaginable defiance. Only the mind-numbing effects of the poison of the gonads coursing through their brains could have made them decide to give women the vote. We *told* you it was diabolical. This manual is *not* for the squeamish!

During World War II, women became an integral part of the work force. The men were overseas fighting the war, so someone had to man the jobs here at home. Does *Rosie the Riveter* ring a bell? That seemingly innocent, small taste of what it was like to be men was intoxicating to the previously easily controlled women; they soon realized something had to be done to alter the status quo. That something was an insanely clever, insidious, multi-pronged attack on the very fabric of our society.

Our research leads us to believe that The Plan was cleverly put in place during those mandatory, yet seemingly clandestine sixth-grade sex-education classes. They conveniently separated the sexes to graphically explain the physical functions of human reproduction.

As if the boys needed to know how our little members became such magnificent stiffies. Most of us were probably thinking we don't care, just tell us where to put the damn things! We just wanted a chance to get back together with the girls and demonstrate our newfound knowledge. Of course, the sharing of this new and potentially volatile information with the opposite sex was strictly forbidden. Many of us thought it strange that they would show us all this cool stuff with filmstrips, pictures, and slides, then expect us not to put the knowledge to use. The question was essentially: why bother? It's just going to frustrate us. The answer was that the female instructors were teaching the girls the same thing at the same time, but with an emphasis on how to frustrate boys. Boys who would become men.

We can just picture a frumpy old-marm of a school teacher, in a daisy-print, buttoned-up to the neck shirt, with lace on the collar and wrists, standing at a chalkboard with the words: SEX EDUCATION written at the top of the board. She's drawing represenations of male and female anatomical structures; most of which she has neither seen or touched in person. She knows exactly how to frustrate boys and girls, and has been doing so for decades. She is a perfect example, and implement of their sinister plot.

There was one major difference in the delivery of the routine presentation given to the girls though, they incorporated, THE PLAN.

Their plan is to make men so placid,

that soon all guys would be flaccid.

Once proud, strong and virile men,

now mere sheepish little runts.

A plan devised and staged then

by dirty little minds.

Obviously conceived by women plotting to overthrow the natural order and install themselves as rulers of the world, this insidious scheme equipped the blossoming life-crushers with the information, strategies, and skills they would need to confuse, control, and conquer men. All future generations of men would know frustration.

What's more, they've been secretly teaching The Plan to schoolgirls for the past six decades; maybe longer. Our Research and Development team postulates that their movement may have roots all the way back to Ruby Magdalene, founder and proprietor of Ruby's House of Forbidden Pleasures by the Sea. Being Mary's elder sister, she may have trained her younger sibling to infiltrate the male-only power conglomerates of the era. She is believed by some to have been as shrewd and cunning as any man of the day. The movement may have been inspired by her obvious success.

It may have taken centuries, but once they had enough young impressionable females brainwashed and indoctrinated into their way of thinking, they put The Plan into action.

They launched the Sexual Revolution; a revolting campaign that they would eventually win! Throughout the decades that followed, the battle raged, with men becoming ever more weakened, giving up and giving in at an ever-increasing rate. It was the battle of the sexes. And men, we got our asses kicked!

We really didn't know what was happening. It all happened so fast, sounded so great: Free love, what a great idea! The Pill, sexual freedom, burning bras, and independent women being viewed as sexy, all contributed to men slowly but surely relinquishing their dominion over women. All the while we thought we were demonstrating our masculinity! Part of the plot.

Then came popular songs and films depicting women as strong heroines; no, now it was heroes, actors not actresses, the changing of our language to be *politically correct,* little girls in Little League, the growth in popularity of soccer, Title 9, shattering the glass ceiling, women as CEO's, it was all too much! As a group, women became stronger and stronger, and began exerting their will onto our culture. We did not know how to fight it until it was too late. The damage was done. We didn't stand a chance. It was full-blown pussoppression!

Look inside any corporation in America today and you will find a certain, oh-so-familiar feminine touch contaminating the way business is conducted. It's especially pervasive in Human Resources where the touchy-feely approach to communication in the workplace permeates the air like the stench of a hair salon.

Managers can no longer control their subordinate's behavior and expect actual results. No, they must *understand* the employee, *empathize* with the employee's situation, *counsel* and *nurture* the employee. Excuse us while we barf!

This is our darkest hour. We face our most daunting task. We must regain our manhood! It won't be easy, they have burrowed into every nook and cranny of our society, spewing forth their anti-male venom with such ferocity and guile that men are afraid to act like men. Any act of masculinity is looked upon with scorn and contempt. Most males have simply given up, clearly we cannot even consider them to *be* men any longer. Bad news guys: there are no certificates for participation, it's competitive out there!

Now, we're not talking about quiche eaters or the pull-my-finger Sluggo types of stereotypical males, we mean the type of men who know how to treat women, know how to please women, and know how to control women. Men who understand women; men who know and can give women what they want without sacrificing their man-sacks to the goddess of femininity. Maybe you can be one of us: the few, the bold: The Testicled!

Men such as these are the types that one might see lounging at the beach wearing sunglasses that people think hide the fact they are scoping out babes in bikinis. They don't care, they pull their shades down on their noses whenever a particularly attractive sun worshipper passes by. They appreciate beautiful women on the beach in bikinis. If they didn't, women wouldn't spend billions of dollars each year on being a beautiful woman on the beach in a bikini. But they do, so…

These men have shown they have the required qualities to become Members of the All-American Man Club, or AAMC.

♂ Much has been written and said about the phenomenon known as Mansplaining, the practice of men explaining subjects to women in a condescending manner. Far from what most women perceive as demeaning, or as a male character flaw, our members engage in this activity solely out of a genuine concern for the well-being and edification of women. Would women rather have us explain things to them in a vicious, threatening manner? Of course not, and that is not what we at the All-American Man Club advocate.

Let's face facts, many, many subjects need to be explained to some women, not all women, but some. The world is a very confusing place, and men are simply trying to assist the women that do need help navigating the treacherous waters of life. The way we think of this subject is: You can mansplain to all women some of the time, to some women some of the time, and to some women all of the time, but not all women all of the time. It's just a matter of into which category the woman to whom you are mansplaining falls.

Let me mansplain for those of you who need further clarification, (ladies, you know who you are) complicated means there are many inter-related factors involved, and not all women can always take care of themselves. That's when it's good to have a man around who can guide you through the tribulations— that means experiences that test your patience, endurance or faith. Just think of us as male lions in a pride, we don't do much except eat and mate, but we're sure good to have around when hyenas are lurking about.

And speaking of the natural, animal kingdom, don't be misled by the misguided information placed out there in recent times.

♂ Some woman who says she's some sort of doctor wrote a book offering sex advice to every creature, or some such nonsense. Let's call her Dr. Lotts. We're not sure who she plans on having read the book, since by our estimation, zero animal species can read, and probably about the same number need any sex advice.

She claims that in more than 80 species, females eat their mates before, during, or after sex. What we want to know is: Doesn't devouring your intended mate before, as in *prior to,* sexual intercourse sort of interfere with the act itself? After all, a lot of good can be accomplished with just some steamy porn and a handful of K-Y, but it usually takes two to mate!  Unless she's referring to single celled organisms that propagate their species asexually, we just don't understand the relevance. Now granted, with Members there is often a significant amount of eating that takes place prior to the actual consummation of the act, but somehow, we just don't think that's what the sweet little, misguided doctor lady meant.

♂ ♂ ♂

♂ *The reason those vacuum-seal food saver devices are so popular with so many housewives has nothing to do with convenience or saving money. There is just something about the concept of sucking the life out of things and putting them to use later that appeals to the nature of women.*

CHAPTER THREE:
FEMICOMMS AND ENTERTAINMENT

Why do women thoroughly enjoy any commercial that eviscerates men? They see every commercial that insults the masculine characteristics that define men as an instant classic. Women everywhere can be seen snickering, casting sideways glances at their meek mannered men as they unilaterally embrace the latest product of the Gelding-Maker Machine. When confronted, women say this is only harmless joking. They take particular delight in watching men squirm when viewing a commercial that can be related directly to their mate. Each one, another scissor-snip on the old man-sack. Harmless?

With men, not so much. Men don't want or need to belittle women. Men really just want to see T & A.

Big T; Tight Little A.

Preferably in skimpy little dental floss style bikinis, handing out ice cold beer, and frolicking on the beach. We do so enjoy a good frolic. And big T.

Do you know what T&A is? Right, but also Wrong! It's a clever ruse, an advertising term that means: What guys will watch for more than 10 seconds during the game's TV timeout. It's also the answer to the advertiser's dilemma, "How do we keep them in front of the 'T-tube' during commercial breaks?"

By the way, here's a tip for everyone who is involved in producing those classic, if misdirected commercials, you know the ones; with the big…ti...and… the… bi-kini… and the tight…no!... Must...con…cen…trraaate! Back to business. The tip is: Men do not care what brand of beer you're pushing. We'll still drink whatever brand is available right then and there!

All we want is the fantasy! And not to have to make any decisions. Especially on weekend, or when the game is on.

Also, just so you know, we always drink whatever anyone has. Doesn't mean Jack. We all have our separate favorites, and occasionally, we will try some new red, or imported, or the latest got-to-do-it-to-be-cool beer, but we aren't really swayed by the hum-drum boring ads.

When we run out of our own stock, we'll simply send our women out to get more. That way we still won't have to make a decision. If there are no women around to service us, we'll just buy the brand we always buy. So, stick with the clinically enhanced swim teams and frolicking beach parties. That's what gets us hot enough to have another ice-cold brew. Did we mention big T?

But that's not what we get. All too often commercials are designed to insult that which makes us men, and only serve as vehicles to spread the female's anti-male propaganda. We can just imagine the next "perfect" example of feminine-biased commercials, or femicomms as we call them here at The AAMC HEAD-quarters, we love calling it that. The eviscerating ad would probably involve two attractive, seemingly harmless, buxom young women exiting a street-side café and discussing--quite naturally--feminine hygiene. Our guess is feminine odor, along with laundry additives, must rank as the most popular subjects among women in the 18-50 life-sucking demographic. Their conversations seem to center around these subjects quite often.

As the two go around the corner, they are, as if part of a quite ordinary situation, confronted by the stereotypical exhibitionist flasher; trench coat at flash-ready. With unabashed enthusiasm, he thrusts open his coat in gleeful, if perverted, anticipation that his victims will be sent fleeing, screaming in abject terror. Instead, they remain calm, collected, and of course, lemony fresh!

They coolly look down, and staring at the would-be assailant's surprise package, one of them states with calm detachment, *"That reminds me, I need to get the family photo enlarged."*

To which the other dispassionately adds, *"Yeah, I need to pick up some Vienna Sausages."*

Much laughter, another big hit, an instant classic with all the women. They'll probably air the affront during the Super Bowl telecast.

If it degrades men, even the perverts, they'll love it! The airwaves are saturated with these femicomms, so be ready. The next time she starts to snicker in your direction after being exposed to a femicomm degrading men or depicting a male committing a feminine act, be polite, but warn her to tread lightly since tongues were made for speaking with respect to each other, not necessarily for licking!

Movie Rating System

The current movie rating system is woefully inadequate since it disregards a certain critical element. The single most important factor to our Members is the femininity factor.

We couldn't care less if a movie is rated G or R, this means nothing to us. Well, almost nothing; we do appreciate a good R or XXX rated film from time to time. Anyway, what this country needs is a new "F" category of ratings for the mounds of movies that embody the true spirit of femininity, yes, the dreaded Chick Flicks.

Have you ever been duped into watching at least part of one of these mush bombs? Say, when one of your clever, conniving co-ed so-called friends entices you into downloading the film because it's supposed to be hilarious. You get your popcorn and sit back waiting for the film to, for lack of a better term, become funny. After a few minutes of estrogen-laced male bashing, through which she is afflicted with uncontrollable giggles, you begin to realize that the joke is on you. This alleged comedy is a thinly-disguised taco fest. Yep, a chick flick.

When the hapless male lead character goes to the drug store trying to purchase feminine hygiene products, professing his true and undying love for her, and trying to convince her to forgive him for whatever ungraceful sin he committed, you realize you'll never reclaim those wasted moments of your life. You tried to tough it out but are compelled to run, screaming from the room, searching for any vestige of masculinity to save you from plunging into an estrogen induced coma. To save our

Members from this disastrous situation, we suggest adding an entirely new category to the canon of ratings. We want an "F" rating placed on every chick flick. We recommend the following rating criteria:

F: Contains content that may not be conducive to masculine behavior. Minimum requirement for all chick flicks.

FE: Chick flick with high estrogen content. Masculine guidance suggested. Not suitable for younger male audiences.

FU: Films that are disguised as comedies or action flicks to fool men. Watching these can cause menstrual cycle synchronization.

EF: Reserved for egregiously feminine films. Caution: Viewing these fem-films can cause unsightly swelling of male breast areas and substantial shrinkage of the gonadal cluster.

FFF: Banned Films. Contain blatant femininity, graphic male subservience, and wanton disregard for true male status. Intentional viewing of films in this category will result in the loss of your manhood, self-esteem, and Man Card.

♂ ♂ ♂

♂ *Beware your steps, your gaze, your casual tongue moving you ever closer to the abysmal dwelling place of the soulless eunuch.*

CHAPTER FOUR:
CURSES AND LISTS

The Ever-Present Lists

Men are under a constant barrage of lists women produce, lists that serve as not too subtle reminders of how little regard some women have for men. The internet provides daily prodding designed to castigate and subjugate men. It's all part of their plan. We at the All-American Man Club take umbrage with these lists, as they promote the female agenda, but do nothing but harm to the master gender. Here are some examples, ripped from the home pages on internet browsers of unsuspecting males.

Ten Things You Should Never Say to A Woman

Before we make the descent into women's attempts to control our behavior, we need to understand that the typical reaction of most AAMC members when confronted with any list of supposed acceptable behaviors is to scoff, deflect, and try to help the poor, misguided little dears find their true place in life. We stand ready to assist.

Among the banned items on the list are common sense missteps that most men avoid like that moody girl on the beach, sitting alone and popping Midol pills as though they were candy. Men instinctively know not to ask if women are *PMSing* as that particular foray into Hell can result in anything from enduring a visceral tirade demeaning your manhood, to an actual physical assault wherein she tries to "de-man" you. Our advice: You don't need our advice on this one, you know better. Don't go there, save your sack. More on this later.

Next comes a compilation of taboo statements that, if dared to be voiced, will result in public evisceration as women attempt to shame men with the ubiquitous "ooooooooh."

Men are reminded in these pointed and biased articles not use the terms: *Because you're a woman; Let a man do that for you; Like a girl; and No place for a woman.* These statements don't disparage women, rather, they express the natural desire men possess to protect the weaker sex. As is the case with so many other frowned-upon, yet innocent statements, these innocuous terms aren't meant to deride, but just to offer services where and when needed. Why is it that women seem to want and admire a hero, but balk at men who are only trying to fulfill their genetic obligations to women?

Other statements men should never dare make to women include:

Smile: how can that be such a bad term? Everyone loves to see someone smile, that's when we know someone feels good. People are universally recognized as more attractive when they smile. Geez, try to accept that men don't have an ulterior motive for wanting women to look their best and be happy.

Don't Be So Bossy: This seems obvious. Again, we are only looking out for women when we say this because, let's face it, it's a man's world out there. If women want to fit in to the workforce, being bossy is NOT going to help. And remember, what was the name they gave that unpleasant cow? That's right, Bossy!

Just sit there and look pretty: Ref: Smile. Same response, we like it when women are pretty, and we believe women don't want to sit there and look ugly. The multi-billion dollar a year make-up business stands as a shining example of how and why women need to conceal their true nature. They're consumed with trying to sit there and look pretty. We deeply appreciate their time and effort, so don't judge us by a flawed standard.

That's not ladylike: Well, some things women do *aren't* ladylike. But who's to say that's a bad thing? Many men want their ladies to be a little less prim and proper from time to time. On the other hand, ladylike refers to a specific mode of behavior that has been deemed socially acceptable for generations. So, this term shouldn't even be included here.

And finally, the question, *you like sports?* is as natural a response as anyone can imagine when, after decades of derisive comments, rolling eyes, and total disdain for man's obsessive interest in sports, we find a rare, female sports fan. Forgive our surprised reaction, but our actual thought process is about how hot the woman is, and not what the correct reaction should be.

On the other side of the proverbial coin, the side that does not contain *tails* and as such should rightfully be ignored, are the myriad things women wish their men would do. Oh, how special. Our emotionally challenged R&D department calculated the number of things men wish women would do. The answer referenced the number of stars in the Milky Way. So, that's probably a lot, because math doesn't lie! Nobody mentions that.

All the usual complaints were listed in this article. The whining list included, but was not limited to:

Finish the laundry: Hey, we didn't start the laundry, why should we finish it?

Write random love notes: What am I, Dante Alighieri? Vinnie Van Gogh? What's next, you want me to snip off some part of my body to go with my sack?

Get in on meal planning: EZ, cook me a big steak, get me a beer!

Point out what she's doing right.   ……still waiting…..

Make a wish list: See Honey-Do lists.

Hug without expectations: Can't be done. It's just not natural.

I should treat myself; give more back rubs: All result in the same activity. You know what I like, and I'm up for it anytime! Be careful what you wish for.

Wear the shirt she bought me: Don't buy me lavender shirts that match the ones you wear. Look, we'll wear anything you bought that we preapproved, but when you go rogue and buy some dipstick looking outfit that makes us look like teen idols, that crap is going to stay in the closet. We're MEN dammit, Members of the All-American Man Club, not pre-drop members of a boy band or members of the unified eunuch guild!

Change a diaper—or three. You know it makes me gag! Why put us through that, WE didn't feed the kid. Typical, not just one diaper, the demand instantly jumps to three. Give an inch…

Talk: Sure, let's talk about the poor guy whose woman wrote this list. He *needs* to become a member.

Say thank you: Okay, sure, if it makes you happy, "Thanks."

Honey-Do Lists

Have you ever seen the commercial that shows some guy sitting down to watch a football game, but his wife has changed the access code via the parental controls on the remote? He can't watch the game until he finishes his list of wife/ruler-appointed chores, known to lesser souls as the Honey-Do List. Mr. Eunuch sits there and succumbs to the obviously superior power of his Master's whip.

Well, guess what the result would be if that was attempted in an All-American Man Club Member's home.

That's right! He would calmly, in a deeply, guttural Hannibal Lecter tone of voice, explain to her that the remote controller, which she had no right to even have in her possession in the first place, would be handed over within about four seconds; along with the access codes. And God help her if any of the game was missed! He'd let her know that if the remote wasn't returned to its rightful owner in the time allotted, then the taxi to take her to her mother's house or any ex-boyfriend's place would be on the way in the very near future!

Members know honey-dos are merely a woman's attempt to communicate their intended but coded message to a man. The message is coming in loud and clear; *I'm in charge, and if you behave, you just might get your testicles back tonight for your weekly fifteen minutes of shame.* Those minutes will include the expected standard 12/3 ratio; that is 12 minutes of prep work-- you know you can't skip the pre-lims and go straight to the main event without enduring her post-coital repercussions--and your three minutes of hard work. Go ahead, bang away lover boy.

To fight back, Members have developed a Honey-Do list for her:

- ✓ Shut Up
- ✓ Lube Up
- ✓ Bend Over
- ✓ HANG ON!
- ✓ Get me a beer

THE Curse

You went there anyway, in spite of our warning. Ok, you made an honest effort; even though you promised yourself it wouldn't happen, it did. You dutifully practiced harmless, innocuous responses to open statements that begged for smart-ass responses, but to no avail. When it came to crunch time, you forgot all your careful preparations, and you made the near-fatal mistake of making a caustic comment about her monthly excursion to Bitchland on the PMS Express.

You moron.

Don't look at us, we're not dumb enough to say something like that to her face. Sure, we Members have a bit of a cavalier attitude, and an "I did it, what about it? Get me a beer" approach to domestic squabbles, but we're not taking the fall for anybody who crosses that line.

Of all the taboo subjects you can broach, the one that will catapult her into an explosive rage and scuttle you into the depths of a sexual abyss, is any reference to PMS and her resultant, let's say, less than sunny disposition.

But you're not alone. As men, we often cannot stop ourselves from taking these quick, easy shots that undermine her womanessense. Yeah, it's a new word. We made it up, what about it? Get me a beer.

Anyway, men throughout time have been plagued by the curse of the monthly visitor every bit as much as women. It's probably traceable all the way back to cavemen, and of course, cavebeeaatches.

We're pretty sure--at least our crack research department tells us--it is quite possible the following scenario was played out in monthly cycles in ancient caves from Ethiopia to France to Mazatlán.

Old Bonk comes in from a rough day of hunting in the wilds and says quizzically, "What in the name of the Great Ball of Fire in the Sky is that smell?"

To which his cave mate Gronnika responds, "Have you smelled your sorry pelt lately, you miserable sloth-humper?" Or words to that effect.

Not one to back down from a lowly female, Bonk shoots back, "At least a sloth will move around once in a while!"

This only serves to incite poor suffering Gronnika further. "Oh I know you di-int. How DARE you come up in here, not in MY CAVE, talkin' 'bout smells and sloths and…! I KNOW you ain't talking 'bout me! Oh no; Oh Hell no! I'll show you, you little wimpy-ass, can't find no job, knuckle-dragging, worthless, piece of…" and grabs a big rock, with the intent to make a permanent rearrangement of Bonk's facial features.

You see at this point, Gronnika, having had her fill of Bonk's complete insensitivity in her time of special need, has decided that her man, the man who has literally brought home the bison, is now going to be relieved of his gift of life; he needs to die. She launches a vicious full frontal attack that leaves the thick-skulled Bonk genuinely fearing for his life. Fun fact: Her agitated state of mind would later come to be known as going bonkers.

He is overcome and has absolutely no recourse. His only hope for survival is to grab his club and relieve the menstruating mad woman of her consciousness. Without a doubt this was accomplished with the aid of his wingman, who handed him the club. Then, being the official artist of the cave, captured the moment on the cave wall. Thanks to the wingman's artistic skills and poor timing, the only image to survive to modern times was that of old Bonk carrying his life-saving club over his shoulder and dragging his nearly comatose tormentor by the hair back to her temporary resting place.

Thus was born the misconception that cavemen found it necessary to bludgeon their would-be mates into submission. The truth is, it was self-defense. Of course, he makes every effort to ensure that she is cozy and comfy during her four to seven-day monthly siesta. He thoughtfully stays by her side the entire time. She might awaken and need to be re-convinced.

During this time, he experiences the natural urges any man would face in a similar situation. He hungers, he has needs; after all he *is* a man. He has a huge headache pounding in rhythm with his heartbeat, and a small amount of food on hand, but he can't leave her alone so he busies himself practicing mock combat and hunting skills. Much like a modern martial artist or shadow boxer, he practices techniques in the air against imaginary mastodons, saber tooth tigers and other cave-dweller foes.

He realizes that, although he has his mate lying in a stupor right in front of him, the flowing river of non-conception prevents him from enjoying the company of his mate. He passes the time by exploring his masculine side. Eventually, he pleasures himself.

And there you have it. Now you know the true origin of two insanely popular activities. In one fell swoop, Old Bonk managed to invent Cave-Bo and masturbation. Not a bad week's work.

♂ Love a woman for her personality. They each have about nine or ten so you can just pick one.

♂ *Welcome to the darker side of Man. Where Evil laughs at the righteous.*

CHAPTER FIVE: ABERRATIONS

Perhaps the most dangerous threat to mankind, and the latest example of the ongoing efforts of women to undermine our way of life and dominate men the world over, is the emergence of Metrosexuals. This travesty has been manufactured and perpetrated on our society by clever advertisers, mostly PR women, and embraced by the feminine, gender-friendly media.

Imagine, men who prefer an afternoon at the salon to an afternoon in the park throwing the football around, or to an early morning on the bank of your favorite fishing hole. Can you picture men getting their faces exfoliated, their spiked and tussled coifs highlighted, and their bodies wrapped in an unholy concoction of mud and pickle juice?

This very procedure was unashamedly displayed for all to see, yes, even the children, on public television not long ago. A technician was shown rubbing a thick, creamy, sticky, white substance all over the welcoming back of an openly self-admitted Metrosexual. It looked like a porn film money shot gone horribly, horribly wrong.

Now, we're not saying that men, in general, couldn't use a little more culture or refinement. We appreciate that an afternoon at the museum can enrich and enlighten. Certainly, there is time in every man's schedule for the pursuit of knowledge. However, these outings can and should be scheduled during the off-season of a man's favorite sport, thereby not interfering with one of his primal passions. No harm, no foul.

But that is completely different from men spending the day having their nails done, picking out just the right moisturizing crème for their inner thighs, and getting that wholly disgusting, vomit-inducing jizz rub.

Men are not supposed to enjoy these activities, and certainly, no card-carrying Member of the All-American Man Club would consciously choose a mud bath over mud wrestling. The guys that do enjoy these types of blatant feminine acts are about one genome shy of being completely gay, and ruining yet another family's Thanksgiving Dinner by coming out of the closet over the yams.

BTW: What is it about the sight of a glistening hot, fully stuffed, tom turkey lying on its back, with its legs in the air that inspires closet dwellers to finally open up and admit their long, yet repressed love of and desire for some man-gravy? Please don't misunderstand, we don't *care* that they're gay, we appreciate them. Besides, we probably already knew anyway. What we want to know is, why pick that particular time and place to proclaim who you are? Many families live in fear of the Thanksgiving holiday dinner for this very reason.

At least gay guys know who they are and are eventually quite proud of themselves, as evidenced by the numerous parades each year. But not Metros, confusion reigns supreme with this group of guys who can't seem to make a decision.

At the very least, Metro's have fallen prey to the cunning, avaricious advertisers whose sole intent is to sell product. News

Flash Metro's! You've been duped into a lifestyle that not only betrays your brethren; it demonstrates your total lack of ability to think for yourselves.

But, we're here to help. We can illuminate your path and demonstrate how the seemingly harmless choices you make now can ruin your lives forever. To help you understand the devastating effects your neo-feminist behavior has on the few remaining men in this world, we are here to guide you.

Stay At Home Dads (S.A.H.D)

SAHD, pronounced SAD, is perhaps the most accurate acronym ever devised. These guys would rather stay at home, take care of the kids, and let their wives go out and support them.

A television news feature aired a few years ago that detailed this fascinating, if disheartening, phenomenon. Reportedly, one in twenty homes in America has these stay-at-home-dads who have exchanged roles with their wives. The males take care of the children, clean, cook, sew, eat Bonbons, drive all the kids to soccer practice, do the laundry, and have a healthy and wonderful meal all prepared when their hard-working hubbies, oops, sorry, we mean wives, trudge home from another hard day of fighting off the boss's advances and having their obvious talents stared at and probably groped.

Yes, while the wife is out wasting her time bumping her head on the glass ceiling, if not the boss's desk, and winning the bread, the SAHD guy is content to remain in the safety of the humble, lemony-fresh abode, baking the bread, scrubbing the carpet where little Peter Jr. pee-peed and trying to keep up with who cheated on, killed, plotted against, laid, insulted, deceived, had arrested, ran away from, ran off with, or had the baby of whom on his favorite "daytime drama." A soap opera by any other name...if you prick us do we not... fall into a hopeless, overtly over-dramatized social death spiral brought out by our inherent personality flaws?

Another frightening fact reported was that forty per cent of the alleged men surveyed responded that they would be willing to exchange roles and be a SAHD if their wives' wages alone would be enough to cover their family's financial needs. Of course they want to change places with their wives, it would give them a chance to finally wear the pants.

What in the hell happened in this country?

Where did all the MEN go? It is obvious that the number of Men in this country is dwindling. We fear that as our dads and granddads, the so-called Greatest Generation, dies off, there won't be enough Men left to fight off the evil female plot of total world domination.

Although these guys went off to war and opened the door for the femininity led hostile takeover, it was really the subsequent generations that caved in and allowed women to become the powerful foes they are today. The touchy-feely seventies, or as we call it, The Decade of Darkness, with Charlie's Angels, the Captain and Tennille letting love keep us together, and other fem-shows, crushed whatever masculinity men had remaining and ushered in the rise of the force that is: Woman, hear them roar.

What about Starsky and Hutch? Were they gay, or did the writers and producers just like to watch them hug every week? Not that it makes a difference, we just wonder if this was all part of the plan. Now these SAHD bat-rastards want to drive us all further under the female thumb. Hugs are standard greetings in society today. Welcome to our new country; The United States of Geldings.

Not on our watch!

As card-carrying members of the All-American Man Club, we cannot allow this to happen! Men, it is time to act! That which has been bequeathed to us must not be stolen away by the cunning she-devils. Each of us must find the inner courage to do battle with the so-called weaker sex. And that means you may need a little GOYA therapy. This therapy can help you realize that your SAHD life truly is a SAD life, and not one a Member of the AAMC can recommend.

If you are not a bona fide Member of the All-American Man Club and a proud carrier of the All-American Man Card, commit yourself to our noble cause and join us. If you have already answered the call, then go out and recruit others; save someone from the shame and torment of being whipped. Help a brother out.

Be careful with new recruits though. Remember, they have shattered egos, little or no self-respect, and may even be thoroughly brainwashed. Slowly help him off his knees; get him standing tall and erect, walking proud, the way a man should be. If you can't help him, if he is beyond redemption, he will always be one of those sad SAHD FILKs, or Fathers I'd Like to Kick.

And by the way, did Tennille ever let the Captain speak? Did he ever get to mutter even one word? You can google them, but your parents or anyone over forty will know who they were.

♂ Let us set the record straight. Any All-American Man Club Member who does in fact have an erection lasting for more than four hours DOES NOT need immediate medical attention. He doesn't need to see a doctor, he needs to find a cat house! Let him get some immediate oral, or vaginal, or even hand-al attention. And bring him some KY, STAT!

♂ Another one of our Members, who happens to be an atheist, shared this with the Membership at a recent meeting. He was having trouble sleeping and had seen several different doctors searching for the reason. After many fruitless visits, he was finally diagnosed by a psychologist with dyslexia, and of course, insomnia.

Now he knows why he stays awake all night wondering if there is a dog.

♂ If you happen across a woman that claims that chocolate is better than sex, politely suggest that maybe she should try some different candy. Perhaps she should give Mr. Goodbar a shot, and give up the bite-sized mini-bars.

CHAPTER ~~SEX~~ SIX:
WHAT WOMEN WANT

(Did we give it away?)

What women want: perhaps the most sought after yet elusive knowledge in the history of man. We have been seeking the answer to this enigma since the first woman confronted a man with a totally unexpected tirade; over what, the poor guy had no idea. We solved the ancient riddle and are about to reveal one of the most powerful gems of knowledge in the known universe.

Men have never known exactly what women wanted because of the constant, inescapable fluctuations in moods that they seem to experience minute to minute. We ask them what they want and they tell us that we should know. We do what they tell us to do and they jump all over us for not asking how to do the task properly. It seems to us that they are never happy, never satisfied, that they always want what they don't have or what they cannot have.

Some would comically postulate that they want *everything*; that they want it all. In a way, that's true, but just a little simplistic. We believe that what they want lies at the very basis of their existence: To Propagate the Species. They want, nay need, to ensure the survival of the species. Naturally, they will therefore, select the mate that gives their offspring the greatest chance for survival. They search for and ultimately choose the strongest, or smartest, or richest mate they can find. Not only does their selection ensure the best possible offspring, but the fact that they have selected such a powerful mate ensures that they will also secure the most advantageous societal position for themselves. The social position of their mate ensures their own social status. It comes down to this:

Women Crave Power

Real or perceived, in any of its myriad complex manifestations, power is truly what women want. They will eagerly accept it from you; or more accurately, accept it *in* you, provided you are willing to show the world that; One, you have it; and two, they can get it vicariously. If they can't get it from you, they will get it through, over, in spite of, or without you. Their need is real, deep-seated, and inexorably tied to their very existence.

It is in their souls. They need to feel the power.

Power can obviously come in many forms, and can be gained in a multitude of ways. Physical size or prowess can make a man powerful. For some men, the career position they have attained has given them a certain measure of power over their subordinates, while others rely on the power of information and knowledge to secure their niche in the pecking order.

However, absolutely nothing on this earth can match the power of the great equalizer, money. Money makes ugly guys handsome, and beautiful women cheap. Power, quite simply, gives one person control over another.

♂ Side note: While discussing this topic with some of our Members recently, one pious Member stated that we can't say there is nothing more powerful on this earth than money. He claimed that God's Will on earth in much more powerful and has nothing to do with money.

Our response was, "Oh, really? Have you seen the Vatican? There's a small bit-o-change in those halls. Eh, lad?" We'll take the win on the money angle, but even we must acquiesce to the power of God's Will on earth. We don't mind the friendly reminder from time to time, it keeps us on the right path. Besides, we enjoy the fact that our female companions often invoke His name when we're with them late at night.

But back to money and power, two interconnected desires by both men and women. Think about it. Have you ever seen a poor, short, fat, ugly, bald guy with a beautiful woman? Nope. But, give the same guy a couple of million bucks, and babes everywhere will be lining up, begging for a chance to be of service to him!

World renowned golf instructor Jim McClain listed some mistakes that could kill a golf swing as *Death Moves.* Similarly, there are certain mistakes that men can make; certain conditions that men will allow that will most assuredly result in *Death Moves* to their man packages.

Foremost on the list is the tragic and often fatal mistake of turning over control of the checkbook to HER. Any man that abdicates control of the family income and expenses, in essence, the power of the throne not to mention his family jewels, has just sentenced himself to a life of servitude. He should enjoy banging the gong as his master enters the room; that's the only thing they let eunuchs bang!

The principles are simple. Somehow, either through a lack of testosterone or sense, some men simply cannot recognize the inherent dangers in relinquishing their God-given right to rule. Remember, he who has the gold rules. Money is power!

Why do good girls cream over bad boys? Power. Bad boys represent possessing the power to stick it to the man. What girl could resist?

Why does a girl from wealthy family end up, after only two years at a girl's-only college, married to some out of work musician? Because, he has the power to rock her world, and is rockin' it nightly.

Do you think these girls care that they could end up as the night-shift mood enhancers at the downtown sperm bank? Couldn't care less. They want the power that their men can and do supply them. They want it right now, with no regard for the future.

Without fail, when the perception exists that their man lacks power in one form or another, women will seize the opportunity to exert their own sense of power. This power lies dormant in women whose men keep them content. Any sign of weakness will bring their dormant lust for power back to life. Do women gain a sense of power over men knowing they can accuse them of sexual harassment? Of course. So, don't do it, don't give them the opportunity or the satisfaction. Members always avoid this mess.

♂ One of our Members was in a Martial Arts class some years

ago and witnessed the following: The Master was explaining that the origin of power emanates from an area that lies two inches below the navel in a place known as the chi. A particularly attractive young woman stated, almost defiantly, that women actually possess the true power, that it's a little lower, and some people refer to it as the "hoo-chi."

Some women blatantly strut their power over men, and it is unfortunate that many of fall prey to its lure. Other women wait for the right moment to crack the whip over their man's back. This usually happens when his fishing buddies are hanging around; she'll take the opportunity to belittle his rod & reel.

There is a vast web of strategies women employ, but it all comes down to who is in control. It's a constant battle, one from which men must emerge victorious!

Here's the key, women believe they own the most valuable property on the planet. It's prime real estate, enhanced by the law of supply and demand. They know you want to lease the space, either temporarily or long term. Since they are the landlords and decide if you are lease-worthy, they think they have power over you and can dictate the lease terms. You must remain strong and resist the lure of prime real estate. Remember, there is no shortage of rental space in This Man's World! Learn to de-value the property or find some cheaper, less high-maintenance space to occupy.

Women Want and Need Sex, Just Like Us

Most women just don't want to admit it publicly, but the experience must be rousing good sex, not the standard, run of the mill, ordinary boring kind. The kind that leaves men asleep while women search the nightstand for Mr. Ever-ready. It needs to be powerful yet tender, thrilling but safe, and exhilarating but controlled. Watch a firefighter in action sometime, he knows there can't be any indiscriminate pumping or runaway hoses, just the controlled application of resources.

We suggest that if you need to improve your technique, you practice whenever you are alone. Set up a training regimen that incorporates exercises to improve every part of the body you intend you use, and stick to it! Remember, the only way to improve is through hard work, dedication, and hands-on effort.

Now, you might be thinking men are the only gender that thinks about sex all day, every day. Nothing is further from the truth. Well, we do spend an inordinate amount of time on desires of the flesh, but making men think we are the sole gender driven by mad lusting desires was part of their evil plan. Members now know that behind almost every prim and proper scowl lurks a sex fiend waiting for the right man to deliver what she needs.

Women have secretly known for decades that without men, their satisfaction comes down to batteries and latex. These are poor substitutes for flesh and bone. At some point, women need the manly feel of a Member! Our cracked research and development team calculated satisfying the number of frustrated women in the U.S. alone would require enough batteries in one month to power a city the size of Boring, Oregon for a year. But it *is Boring,* Oregon after all.

Their Achilles Heel

Another key strategy in the battle to manipulate, rather than be manipulated by the opposite sex, is to exploit the one glaring weakness they all share. We can take advantage of this flaw in their genetic makeup regardless of how much damage we've done.

Whether you have metaphorically screwed the pooch, or literally screwed the chick at work, you can, with timing and forethought, correct pretty much any mistake you've made by utilizing the knowledge that we are about to share.

So, as either a prospective or a new MEMBER in GOOD STANDING, would you care to take a guess as to *what is* this miraculous gift from Mother Nature? Is it flowers? Can you melt a woman's bitterly frozen heart with an aromatic bouquet from some shop your secretary found online, or for the older crowd, in the yellow pages? Can you douse the flames of fury from a woman scorned by sending her a beautiful sorry-I-cheated floral arrangement?

Thought process tree: Snowballs, Hell, Chances in…

Maybe you think you can win her heart by exposing your feminine side, showing her that you're sensitive and not afraid to cry. Yeah, if so, you've taken your first steps on the road to Eunuchville. Bang a gong, lose your dong, don't get it on.

Or, maybe your ego is telling you that your ability to keep her *satisfied in the bedroom* will keep her in line. What the hell does that mean? Do you let her toss her diaphragm on the nightstand, and karaoke to Shania Twain's *Man, I Feel Like a Woman* while you eat? If that's the case… well, you aren't far off.

Indeed, sexual prowess is of major importance, but you still don't have the answer. You can keep your mate satisfied for a while, and the ability to do so is one of the cornerstone concepts of the All-American Man Club, but it cannot stand alone. The ability to give her the Big-O is a must-have skill; but eventually even making the earth shake won't shake her carefully cultured determination to control you.

Well then, what can?

We recently conducted a query on a major internet search engine for the term *Orgasm* and netted 13,400,000 sites devoted to this elusive quirk of nature. An additional search for the broad topic of sexuality netted 25,700,000 sites. Unbelievable! Thirty-nine million sites devoted to getting either one or both of you to the state of bliss experienced by two or more consenting adults.

But that pales in comparison to what we discovered, and what our regularly high-as-kites research and development staff recognized immediately as the true Achilles Heel of women everywhere.

Okay, okay, we'll tell you.

Our R&D team conducted another search on the same engine and were somewhat surprised to learn that there were a whopping 128,000,000 sites devoted to: CHOCOLATE. Yes, that is one-hundred, twenty-eight-million! That's a 3/1 ratio of chocolate to sex; good numbers. We like things in threes.

Yes indeed! Chocolate, or more accurately their love of it, their devotion to it, and their misery when they don't have it, is the secret to keeping women happy, and healthy.

Don't believe it? Try this: Mention Godiva to a man and he'll most likely conjure up visions of a beautiful naked woman with long blonde hair, riding a horse; lucky horse. Now mention Godiva to a woman. Her eyes will glaze, a faraway stare will cross over her face, her mind focusing only on that dark, velvet-smooth confection. Her face flushes as she envisions her passion, her breathing will become rapid and shallow, and her mouth will become dry. She's ready, and she wants it.

Unless of course you've unwittingly flushed out a lesbian, whose physical responses would be a result of her lusting after Lady Godiva, the bareback rider. No, the common hetero female is fantasizing about a thick, rich bar of world-class creamy or dark chocolate.

Want to bring her back down? Mention Orgasm; she'll probably just look at you and laugh in disgust.

She may even lament something along the lines of, "I'd rather have the chocolate; it tastes better and lasts longer. Besides, I have a much better chance of getting the chocolate." Being the All-American Man Club Member that you are, you confidently pull a piece of chocolate from your pocket, offer it to her with a nice smile, and the confident reply, "You never know when you might get both."

We sense that there remain a few disbelievers out there among you. Oh, you poor miserable lost souls. Have we not shown you the path to redemption? Have we not opened your eyes to the plague that has been visited upon us? Must we suffer further? Have we not had professional women golfers playing in Men's PGA tour events? Do major retail stores not sell men's-cut jeans to women? When was the last time you saw a male flagman?

But let's see if we can convince you of the sweet seductive power of this confectioner's tantalizing delight. Ever hear of the research that made the bold claim that chocolate was good for you? Yes, of course you did, everyone has heard something of the claim; but do you know the truth behind the report? The original study was commissioned by the giant chocolate/candy manufacturer M&M Mars. It was conducted by a female doctor and originally reported by a female journalist. What possible outcome could there have been? Of course, chocolate is good for you! It soothes headaches and other symptoms associated with menstruation; it is a  mood elevator. Now, ask yourself: who needs those?

Men don't. Imagine a bunch of guys hanging out at Hooter's, watching Monday Night Football and mentally undressing the waitresses. Do you think that instead of beer and hot wings they'll order bottled water and a big melty, chocolate fondue fountain? Even Browns fans don't need that much mood elevation. Also, stop for just a moment and consider that women are much like those chocolate fountains that are so popular in buffets across America today. They're beautiful to look at, you become sensually aroused just watching the smooth, creamy, warm and gooey mess cascade down. But remember, when you poke your stick into one, you are sharing the chocolate with everyone who has already had some of that chocolate. Seriously, does that look like something you should be poking your stick into? But women flock to dip in.

Whenever couples breakup, men and women have similar but

gender specific rituals through which they must invariably pass to close that chapter of their lives and move forward. Men get drunk. It's what we do to cope or celebrate. But for women, it's straight to some form of chocolate, often frozen since they can keep enough on hand for such an emergency without eating the entire stash before their next inevitable, emotional setback.

If you remain unconvinced, ask yourself this: Did Forrest's Mama say that life was like a bowl of jelly-beans, a designer bag full of unspecified gems, a Texas Hold 'Em river card? NO, she said, "CHOCOLATES!" They love Chocolate! CHOCOLATE! **CHOCOLATE!**

Remember: three things that women really want are: Power, Sex, and Chocolate. They want, they need, and they can't escape; use this knowledge to your advantage!

♂ However, there is hope. A report surfaced after the 2005 Macy's Thanksgiving Day Parade that a woman and her eleven-year-old sister were injured by one of the parade balloons. The rogue balloon? The M&M Candies balloon. Chocolate fights back!

♂ *Men, there is one mistake from which you might never extricate yourself. It is perhaps the one thing you can do that means the end of social life as you know it. Even if it takes every ounce of strength, every iota of self-control, you must NEVER call her by your ex's name! To do so means unrelenting punishment and ending up as a convert into their religion:*

The Church of the Confiscated Gonads.

CHAPTER SEVEN: THREATENING SITUATIONS

Male Dancers

There may come a time in your life when she wants to attend a show featuring male dancers with a few friends. This can prove to be a sticky little situation. While you may, at first, feel justifiably threatened, you should also recognize that this is another opportunity for you to assert your manhood.

Forget about the well-oiled sleek bodies, forget about the muscles, and forget about them strutting their bulging packages in front of her face. Forget that she bought a seat in the front row where they routinely rub those bulging packages directly onto women's faces, between their breasts, and all over anywhere and everywhere else the women let them. And they do let them!

She'll let them. That's why she's going!

Do not, repeat do not, let this upset you. It is time to be strong. Don't be a whimpering weasel on this. If you throw a jealous fit and forbid her to go, she'll sense that you are weak and have no self-confidence. She'll immediately start exploiting the weakness and sooner or later she will wear you down, and then Bang! There go your testicles, your All-American Man Club membership and your Man Card.

Instead, encourage her to go with some friends. Just before she leaves, take her aside and let her know that you are excited for her to go, that she and her friends need to get out and have a girl's night out. Tell her you know it will get her juices flowing, and you will want to take advantage of her "heightened state." She'll feel you trust her implicitly, and your relationship is strong and beautiful and wonderful and all those BS things that women need. She won't want to jeopardize that. Plus, she will respect your strength and confidence.

Here's the tricky part. Arrange to meet her with or without the friends after the show. Say you want to have some drinks, continue the party, and join in the fun, whatever. Just make sure you make contact not long after the show, you don't want "Buck the Cowboy" or "Sammy the Saturn Rocket" or anyone else to be able to co-mingle with those flowing juices. Should you fail to convince her that she should meet with you after the show to fill her void, just accept that she has other plans for those juices, plans in which you are evidently not included.

In this case grab an ice-cold beer out of the fridge, and throw your favorite porn on the TV. At least you can get some sleep tonight. You have a big day tomorrow, lots to do:

Throw the wench out! She chose "Nick the Policeman" and his big nightstick over me. Piper time! If you play, you must pay!

Start the search for a new principle squeeze.

Notify All-American Man Club HEAD-quarters, and register my bonus points.

Get info on the annual convention in Vegas.

Expanding Horizons

She announces that she wants a breast augmentation that will cost you $8,000. You're a little unsure what to do. Members know that there is no choice. Pay! If you have the money, make the appointment, if you don't have it, borrow it. Promise her you'll set up a savings account. Just get it done. You should be thinking about how those puppies are going to look and feel, not how much they cost.

Just don't go psycho over guys looking at them. Guys are going to look; you would! By the way, *of course* she doesn't mind all those hound dogs staring at the wholesome goodness of her newly enhanced expandamamms. That's why she got them! Don't feel threatened. All the guys that see you with her will be jealous and will wonder what you have that they don't. Just put a confident smile on your face and remember: YOU are the one that will be rubbing your own personally selected body parts all over her personally purchased erogenous parts tonight! It's your money, enjoy those lusciomamms!

42 Days

♂ *Club Member Style. When informed that he would not be able to engage in intercourse with his wife for six weeks following her surgery, one of our Members, with typical Man Club aplomb, calmly asked the doctor, "So, do you have a loaner, or…?"*

This is an edited version of an epic tale sent in to us by one of our original Members. It describes the unholy ordeal of a medically forced abstinence, and the havoc wrought on, not only himself, but his friends and family as well.

It is a sad, desperate, and gruesome tale. One that men, though they fear it and will try to resist, must be made to hear for themselves; if only to prepare them for the possibility that it could one day, saints preserve us, happen to them.

We must caution you, the following narrative deals frankly and openly with subjects and events that can be unsettling, especially to wimpier readers; caution is advised. It begins shortly after he returns home from the ill-fated doctor visit wherein he learns of his sentence for the next 42 days. The doctor has informed him that due to his wife's surgery, he will not be able to know her in a carnal way for at least the next 42 days. Here is his reaction, shared with the Members:

"Hey Members! Sure enough, the doc said no banging for six weeks!" Oh, the humanity! Can you just hear the anguish in his message? *"But, no problem, I have some great porn, a nudie bar ten minutes down the street, and two good hands, I'm good to go! Now, somebody get me a beer!"*

What bravery, what dedication! This world needs more men of his caliber, men who can adapt, men who can face and overcome even the most grueling challenges with unbridled courage and resolve.

The world needs more All-American Man Club Members!

♂ An observant Member relayed a recent list on the internet detailing seven phrases that ruin relationships. Our initial reaction was that the women referenced in the article were just over-reacting, like they always do. It's so typical, they're just like their mothers, they always do it. Besides, what about all the times they say something like, "I'm fine" when you know they aren't.

Then we saw the seven phrases on the list: *You're over-reacting; You always…; You're just like…; Yeah, well you…; I told you…; I'm fine…;* and *I'm sorry, but…*

Okay, so maybe we might be just a bit guilty on this one. I'm sorry, but what about the phrases they always use to irritate us? Yeah, what about when they say, "Not tonight, I have a headache." Or, "You know that lawn isn't going to mow itself." Let us not forget the dastardly, "Keep up that attitude, dude, and you'll never get your threesome going."

♂ Society without principles is like oceans without fish, religion without a deity, porn without the money shot.

CHAPTER EIGHT:
AAMC GUIDING PRINCIPLES

The Fish in the Sea Principle

One basic principle of the club that every Member needs to fully understand is that there are many, many fish in the sea. Sure, we know you've heard this old saying long before now.  The problem is that too many males don't really believe that, as the axiom implies, there is virtually a limitless supply. Or, they don't believe that they can land that big catch. Indeed, romantic lore is rife with stories of, and references to, the one that got away.

This usually leads to men either willfully or unknowingly subjecting themselves to the ruthless rule of women. Being afraid that the one they're with is the only one for them; they surrender their manhood and end up wearing matching lavender sweaters to the mall on Saturday. Well, *men*, guess what? Take a quick trip to a nightclub, a health club, or the supermarket, and you'll discover why we Members have no fear of losing the one we're with. The supply is endless! They are there, dancing and drinking, sweating through Tae-Bo, Pi-Yo and Zumba workouts, and picking out the biggest and firmest cucumbers in the pile. Plus, they all have one thing in common; they're looking for men!

Whether they're single or not doesn't matter, they are on the lookout. They all share a single driving need, a MAN! If they already have one, they're searching for a better one, if they don't currently have one, the need will be even greater.

So, lose the fear. Grab your poles, put on your rubber waders and do some fishing. You might just land one you can mount!

When you dump the old carcass, none of this wimpy-ass *it wasn't you, it was me* BS! Do both of you a favor and tell that it was her. If it had been you, she would have thrown you out! Don't make the mistake of trying to spare her feelings, you'll only be granting her license to pull the same crap with the next guy. Do us all a favor. Who knows, maybe she'll change her ways and become the servile mate you always hoped she'd be. Or, maybe she'll take a cold, hard, honest look at herself and realize what a pain in the donkey she was. Then, with any luck, she will be a better companion to the next man in her life. Either way, you can take solace in the knowledge that in some small way, you will have contributed to the overall health and well-being, and betterment of the animal known as *man*.

Then go out and celebrate! Your manhood is intact, and you've helped make the world a better place! Welcome to the Revolution!

The Last Boyfriend Principle

We often use the knowledge of this principle as a source of strength whether it's during a first encounter, or in the middle of a full-blown--we love that term--relationship.

Think about this: You spotted the target du' jour at the beach, or nightclub, and you've made it past the awkward first-line stage. She's single, sleek, firm and pouty. You're thinking you'd like to take her out for a test drive; meanwhile she's been busy sizing you up as a potential mate. At this moment, it is important to remember the Last Boyfriend Principle, which states: *Okay, she is attractive, adult and single. But why is she single? It's because her last boyfriend wouldn't put up with her* $#!+.

He obviously understood the Fish in The Sea Principle and made the right decision; he kicked her to the curb! It is now up to you as to how to proceed. By remembering this principle, you can act from a position of confidence at the very onset of the potential relationship, and gain the upper hand.

If you've already been in a relationship for some time, use this principle to turn the tide in your favor. Remember, unless you're picking up fourteen-year-olds, (if so, you sick bat-rastard: see side note below) she's already had a previous boyfriend. Draw strength from the knowledge that if one of your oppressed brothers can dump her, then so can you. Then, refer to the Fish in the Sea Principle.

We know that you may be feeling a bit of remorse, and may be wondering if you have treated her just a little too harshly. This is normal. You don't want to become so bitter and cold that you feel nothing; or worse, derive any pleasure from someone else's misery. So, go ahead, splurge; give her cab fare and an extra five bucks for a pint of chocolate mocha ice cream. That should ease her pain and salve your conscience. It's a win-win.

Side note: If you are an adult and are interested in any young underage females, put down this manual, pick up a dull knife, go outside and cut off your hangers. Not only are you NOT All-American Man Club material, you're not even a man. You don't deserve to reproduce.

The Form and Function Principle

There is a reason why rockets are shaped like phalluses; there is a reason why space shuttle cargo bays display vulvar characteristics. Form fits function. Rockets must penetrate the atmosphere and thrust their payloads deep into space. Shuttles are the vessels that carry and ultimately deliver the cargo.

The countdown is met with great anticipation but must proceed with cautious at first, wary of any detail that could scrub the mission. The rockets ignite and liftoff begins. Speed increases as the fuel burns hotter; at each stage the thrust grows stronger. The rocket reaches its maximum speed just as it reaches escape velocity. Then, with a final tremendous burst of energy, the rocket reaches its destination and delivers its payload.

Having spent its fuel and serving no further purpose, the rocket falls away and drifts off. There is no concern for the fate of the payload, no lasting commitment or emotional attachment; there is only calm, a satisfied detachment at having performed the function for which it was designed.

The space shuttle quite naturally assumes a position revolving around the earth, awaiting the proper time to deliver its cargo. When the time comes, as it must, the shuttle spreads open its doors and delivers the cargo into the cold, harsh environment. Thus, not only completing its assigned mission, but also confirming that, once again, things are right in the universe.

The Men Engage in Manly Pursuits Principle

Every man has his strengths and weaknesses; his likes and dislikes. Some enjoy golf, while others prefer baseball. There are hockey nuts and those whose passion is hunting. Many of us love to fish, yet others find a day at the racetrack exhilarating. We don't all enjoy the same activities, and we might even dislike some that others could not live without.

After all, not everybody loves football. No, wait! That's a bad example. If someone doesn't like football, there may indeed be something wrong with him. That's the one exception. The point is that these are all manly pursuits, and we can all accept that as gospel. So, provided it doesn't involve spending Saturday afternoon deciding what facial moisturizer will give you that special glow, whatever you choose to do to maintain your testosterone level and get some alone time is great. More power to you.

There is, however, one pursuit for which all men share an equal passion. It unites us as a gender. That is the pursuit of knowledge. Keep in mind that knowledge is power, and that all women crave power; they are drawn to it like men to Super Bowl Sunday, MLB Opening Day, or the Daytona 500. Given that, the most powerful knowledge one can attain, and certainly the most rewarding is Carnal Knowledge. Yes, knowledge of the flesh!

So go, get out and recreate. Be manly in your pursuits, whatever they may be. Most importantly, be knowledgeable. Get to *know* many, many women. Forget about our differences, we all seek the same thing, knowledge. Especially the carnal variety.

In fact, if you're ever in one of those awkward moments when you come home really, really late, and she's waiting to ask you where you've been, here's a tried and true saving line many Members have used quite successfully in the past. Simply adopt that far away, dazed look in your eyes and proclaim that you are innocent of any wrongdoing, you were out seeking knowledge.

The Hunt

Another extremely popular and manly activity that is sure to get you out of the house and away from her is hunting.

Plus, you get to wear the coolest camo clothes that make you look like trees. Be careful, some of them make you look like a bush, and that's the target prey of an entirely different kind of hunter.

Hint: If your chosen activity is hunting, try turkey. If you have already tried it, then you know what we're talking about. It's great! There's no tree climbing involved, no hauling huge, smelly carcasses for miles over rough terrain, and dressing a bird is much easier than any four-legged animal, especially when you know the little woman is going to pluck the bird anyway.

A short walk to the hunting area is the only real exercise you'll get, but that can be washed away with a few cold beers later. Then, when you get there, you don't have to go anywhere or do anything. You just lie there like the rest of the vegetation in silence--you do remember silence, don't you--and wait for the ever-wary fowls to wander into the kill zone.

Once the surprisingly intelligent birds are finally in range of your shotgun, you pump them full of copper. You can't use lead, the hole would be too large, and you would ruin the meat. And isn't it the meat we're after? Lead shot used to be illegal due to the poisonous effects on wildlife and runoff rivers, but that's going away. Still, copper is better. You use shotgun shells that are of course, filled with BB's.

We interviewed several turkey hunters in Arkansas, which is, not surprisingly, the turkey hunting capital of the world. On any given Sunday "in-season" you can find groups of turkey hunters in most small towns, gathered around a cooler of beer at the corner convenience store/service station.

At this point, they're easy to spot since their camouflage is less effective against a backdrop of signs that read: BEER WINE CIGARETTES & MILK.

Of course, they have not yet disappeared into the underbrush.

They might not even get to go on an actual hunt that day due to inclement weather or whether they drank too much beer last night. They might just have to hunker down and derive their hunter's satisfaction from sitting around swapping tales about how many beasts they bagged during the Great Rock Creek Turkey Massacre of '97.

Evidently, there are a good many factors involved in deciding whether today is a good day for turkeys to die. Veteran turkey hunters, in the know, won't let you in on all their secrets, but they do point to critical factors such as humidity, wind direction, and whether the little lady at home has any relatives "comin over fer Sundee vis-tin."

When you are lucky enough to get to your spot on just the right day, and you bag a big old tom, you're in for one of life's finest treats. Taking the bird home so your mate can clean and pluck it. You might find you'll have to do some of the dirty work yourself beforehand, but the real treat is the first bite of that fried turkey breast. On the Man Club scale of pleasant experiences, it gets an: *"It's so good you want it last just a little bit longer, oh, please, oh, please!"*

Running of the Bulls

Although there are a very small number of women who run with the bulls in Pamplona, Spain, this is a decidedly male endeavor. Ask just about any woman about this and you are sure to get the usual smug, glib references to the correlation between these manly activities and the respective intelligence levels of men and women.

Rather than a question of intelligence, this is about boys becoming men, about men facing and defeating their fears, and about building the self-confidence to face life's many challenges. This is about what makes us men. We admit, there is a fine line between courage and lunacy, but any man who has the courage to run through the cobbled streets in front of twelve tons of angry bovine, face possible death and probable pain, armed only with a rolled-up newspaper certainly deserves his All-American Man Card!

That is precisely why most women do not run with the bulls in Pamplona. Unfortunately, there will always remain those few misguided females who, suffering from acute cases of penis envy, will line up on the streets during the Fiesta De San Fermin and usually just hug the walls safely as the steers and bulls charge past. Another sad example of how women have attempted to invade the masculine domain, but remain consigned to stand on the sidelines and watch, pretending to participate.

Most people do not realize it, but the fact is that Pamplona is merely one of the many cities, towns and villages throughout Spain where this manly challenge is conducted each year. The rite of passage was probably made famous by some fat writer guy with a bunch of spoiled kids; perhaps just trying to escape the doldrums of married life. At least that's the latest theory to come out of our top-notch Research Department. The annual festival of a manly rites is actually run in cities and towns all over the Spain, sans women of course.

There are, however, unconfirmed reports coming out of the region that there is a similar race in a tiny Spanish village far from Pamplona. Apparently, women are allowed, believe it or not, even encouraged to participate in this somewhat diluted version of its male-oriented counterpart.

Women reportedly come from all over Europe and as far away as the U.S. to test their mettle in an event known as *Strolling with the Cows*. This event is evidently quite popular among a certain, undisclosed segment of the female population. Additionally, there also are possibly a number Metrosexuals who also delight in the frolic. We can't say for sure.

We will continue trying to confirm these reports.

The Genetics Principle

In researching material for this manual, it became abundantly clear that there are distinctive gender-specific traits. There are some behaviors exhibited by men that can only be attributed to genetic predisposition.

Naturally, we're not saying that there are no females who display masculine behaviors from time to time. But let's face it; it is men who are channel surfing, demonically in possession of the remote. It is men who will forbear the ragging nag rather than stop and ask for directions. And, it is men who are obsessed with the size of their…TV's.

Conversely, how many women have you ever seen sitting on the couch with their hands down their pants? Men rarely ask if their asses look big--in any pants--and who ever heard of a man being accused of nagging his wife to death?

We can debate free will, Tabular Rasa, the Grand Scheme, and any other theory that one wishes to postulate. But, we have never seen a bunch of older women cruising the strip in convertible 'vettes, their blue hair flapping in the breeze, and their breasts resting on their knees, while they scope righteous dudes. You don't see a bunch of old, fat, bald guys making quilts on the porch, and laughing at how silly the women look! Also, why don't women have a second childhood?

These behaviors are genetic. They aren't learned. Fathers, brothers and uncles don't take young boys aside and tell them, "Boy, don't you ever get caught sitting on the couch without your hands down your pants." It's genetic! Men don't need to pass along the act of feigning confusion in the kitchen to get out of work. Women fake orgasms, men fake not knowing how the damn cheese grater works. It's genetic!

♂ Another gem we heard about from Dr. Lotts: Something about the timing of events for male honey-bees and climax. Seems that when he reaches climax, he explodes. Duuhhh! Hey Lotts, who doesn't?

We've received quite a bit of feedback on this. Seems that most of our Members routinely explode at that moment. For us though, it usually isn't fatal. One of our Members suggested that the honey bee behaves this way because he's sick of living only to serve the Queen Bee. Maybe it's suicide?

Another Member's comment we received enlightened us as to the mathematical probabilities factor involved in the number of species, 80, that engage in the rather macabre practice of devouring one's mate, either before during or after sex. Since there are an estimated 10 to 20 million species on this planet, a mere 80 of them in the Munch Your Mate for Lunch Bunch doesn't do much to put the sphincter pucker on us; especially when HUMANS are not involved in said munching, usually.

Speaking of math, our R&D guys have given much thought to the question of how big is too big…no, wait, that's not right. The actual concept in question is whether or not women should maintain a dominant role in a relationship. Our R&D guys finally stopped thinking about relevant size issues long enough to do the math. Not surprisingly, the results clearly indicate that women should definitely NOT regard males as being in subordinate roles; sometimes subordinate positions are pretty good, but not roles.

Here's the math: We can all agree on the universal mathematical constant. $a^2 + b^2 = c^2$. The letter "a" represents, rightfully so, men. The "a" stands for Alpha, the first, Adam, all things at their beginning before being messed with by women. The "b" represents women, you can assign your own reasoning here, but go with your imagination and use whatever B-word comes to mind as a spontaneous reaction. The obvious remaining "c" represents the communion, not the holy kind, the kind that signifies the coming together of two as one. The fact is that without one or the other, there can be no relationship. So, the math logic as it pertains to relationships, plays out in this manner:

$a^2 + b^2 = c^2$. If, $a < b \neq c$; or, $b > a \neq c$, then, $b \neq a$

Explanation: Take the universal math constant that a^2 plus b^2 equals c^2. If a is less than or subordinate to b, then there can be no c. If b is greater than a, then, again there can be no c. Therefore, "b" (women) cannot equal "a" (men). Amen to that! So, the math proves that women are not greater than men…just wait…in the relationship dynamic. AND, men are not greater than women.

All-American Man Club Members fully support equality for women in terms of political, economic, and employment status issues and opportunities. We support equal pay for equal jobs, but reserve the right to believe that physiologically, men and women's brains are wired differently, and that we were given certain specific parts for specific reasons, we fit together nicely. We are okay with equal; we just don't believe women, in general, will be satisfied until they have placed men under total subjugation. Note: It also follows logically that $a + a = c$ or that $b + b = c$. And THAT's math! You can't argue that.

♂ We instructed our vaunted Research and Development team to scour the internet for any verifiable, bona fide, science that could justify this view. Professionals always deliver, but *we* got this:

Scientists, in all their arrogance, used to tell us humans were the only animals to make love face to face. We're not sure they have met the criteria of following the basic steps of the scientific method.

However, the R&D staff just pointed out another equation, one that men have been fantasizing about for most of their lives: $a + b + b = gt$ (great times). We can't argue with that logic either, so we'll give them this one.

♂ We do have verifiable research that illustrates the reason some men cannot understand women. When men try to pigeonhole women into specific categories of behavior, the results can be disastrous. Case in point: A man, not one of our Members, recently went to a bar known to cater to females of the lesbian persuasion. His presence had little effect on the patrons who were enjoying their night out, and seemed to be either tolerating or ignoring him completely. He soon tired of his non-affect and decided to change the dynamic to show these lap-lickers just who was who in this life.

Standing on the bar, he called out, "All of you are just women who don't what it's like to have a MAN inside you. Well, I AM a MAN!" The bar fell silent, somber as the women watched his tirade. "In fact," he added, "I like doing exactly what you like doing! I challenge anyone in here to try to do it better than I can! I'll bet a hundred bucks I can outlast anyone in here!"

The club bouncer, a muscular, massive man who stood about six-feet, six-inches in height and weighed-in about a biscuit short of three-hundred pounds, had been standing quietly in the shadows, patiently watching the man, waiting for the inevitable moment when the man would push a little too far and need to be removed. Holding a twelve-inch strap-on in his hand, the bouncer made his way to where the boisterous troublemaker stood and said, "I'll take that bet, come with me."

The color left the man's face as the bouncer helped him down from the bar top. He felt a sudden urge to complain, but the expression on the bouncer's face halted the idea before he could mouth the words. He felt, at once, fortunate to be able to control his tongue, trepidation at what festivities the bouncer had planned for the remainder of the evening, and shame from the hysterical laughter of the women in the bar. That laughter was the last thing the man heard as the bouncer escorted him into the back room. He knew he was in for a rough night.

AAMC Members don't need to compete with women, they don't need to belittle or bully anyone. Had he been a Member of the All-American Man Club, he would never have entered that bar in the first place. He would have been the type of man who accepted all people for who they are. Gays, lesbians, transgenders, who cares? Our Members treat all people the same, we just prefer heterosexual women. Well, and bi-sexual women, but that's another wish. Had the man been a Member, he would have had an entirely different attitude. He'd also be able to walk around pain-free the next day.

♂♂♂

♂ *Looking for something to do while you're lying there in bed, catching your breath and waiting for the effects of the Viagra to release its stranglehold on your swollen and now raw member? Since you have already thoroughly exhausted your lover, and you know you'll be up for another half an hour or so, why not learn another language?*

CHAPTER NINE:
USEFUL PHRASES

There is a quick and simple, easy-to-learn language that All-American Man Club Members can utilize to respond to a wide variety of requests. No special training or extensive memorization is required. Simple immersion techniques in the true nature of what you are--a red-blooded American male--will make the language come naturally. And isn't coming naturally what we all want?

Here is the new language: *No. Never. Forget it. Not gonna happen. I don't think so. Get serious. Nope. Do I look like I give a rat's ass? Not today; not tomorrow; not ever. Chhyeahh, right. Not likely. When pigs fly. Get off my ass! Yeah, THAT'S gonna happen.* Simple. Feel free to immerse yourself in learning and using these new and effective terms as necessary.

In this section, we present Members with a list of useful phrases that have proven to be most effective at communicating and establishing the correct male/female relationship matrix.

When used in the proper tone, and with just the right timing, these phrases, be they comments, questions, or commands, can have a dynamic effect on your relationship. Regardless of your situation, or the hardships you face, the clever use and proper timing of one of these gems will clearly establish the all-important who's who in your relationship.

Learn them well. Study and practice them until delivering the right phrase at the right moment becomes as natural delivering an air biscuit between the sheets at night. Timing is the key to delivery, so vary the utilization; mix them up a bit.

Practice them aloud only if you must and are completely alone. Remember, *your* testicles are on the line here. It is time to accept responsibility, to take ownership.

Useful Phrases List:

Get me a beer!

What's for dinner?

What stain on the carpet?

Sure, I can help with the dishes. SHERRY, GET IN HERE AND HELP YOUR MOTHER!

No, I wasn't staring at her, I was just thinking, I'm glad *your* butt will never get that big.

Where do you keep the _____? (Insert any kitchen gadget).

Don't those puppies get in the way when you do dishes?

How the hell do you work this thing?

I'm so lucky to have you.

No, I'll drive.

Ghmphet Offmphm myph phacemphh! I camphh breaphhmph!

She means nothing to me!

I was thinking of flying to the Bahamas for our anniversary. With the optional, where are you going?

If you ever, God forbid, passed away, I wouldn't remarry. I'd crawl in a hole somewhere and die. I just couldn't live without you. Important note here: Don't overdo the mushy crap by saying something like I couldn't bear to face another dawn...anything that thick will tip her off.

Hey! You weren't complaining last night!

Of course I care about your feelings. But this is football season! We'll talk in March.

It was the dog!

That's why *we* have the penises.

MMMM, it *is* less filling, and definitely tastes better, well, better than the dinner you massacred last night!

It's genetic. We can't help it.

Hey! God designed us that way. Who are you to question HIS judgment?

Crying won't help you get your way.

Violence never solved anything. Now put down the knife.

When all else fails and you are faced with an impossible predicament, one that calls for tough decisive action, remember those three little magic words that she yearns to hear, and for which she has a desperate need. You'll always treasure the memory of the look in her eyes, the quivering of her lips as you lean in close and proclaim in a soft, firm voice, "*You Gotta Go.*"

Hey, apply the Fish In The Sea Principle and give her the boot, cut her loose, tell her to tell her story walking, send her packing, get the fu…well, you get the picture.

Now go celebrate! Toast the man in you. Grab your pole and do some fishing!

FAQs

Refer to the following handy reference guide for those times when she verbally tries to wrestle away control of your relationship, nay, your very manhood. You know the times we mean. The loaded, no win, no right answer questions that make lesser men squirm uneasily in their tighty-whities. When confronted with this quintessential question, "Do these pants make me look fat?" or any other can't win question, the AAMC Member remains calm and replies from a position of strength with a selection from the following officially approved list:

As opposed to what?

No fatter than you looked yesterday.

I know what you're trying to do; I'm out. Game over.

Define fat. Do you mean kind of chubby or freakishly whale-like?

WHUUOOP! WHUUOOP! Testicle Alarm!!!

I can't answer that on the grounds that I could lose my MAN CARD.

What do I look like, some kind of wussy?

Do you think ANYONE can take the Niners back to the Super Bowl, and win?

Quiet! I'm watching the Cat House Series!

Don't come in here! I'm working on a surprise for your birthday.

Today? This week?

Remember when you promised to love, honor, and *obey*?

How did your last boyfriend answer that? And, where is *he* now?

No, but another coat of paint might keep your skin from showing through.

Practice What You Have Learned

Here are more classic questions that can trip you up and land you in masturbationville if you're not prepared. Practice responding to each question with a selection from the above list, or with some of your own personal favorites.

Do you think she's prettier than me?

Am I really bitchy during that time?

What would you do if I got really fat?

Do you think I'm smarter or prettier?

How many women have you been with?

Which would you rather do, go to a Pro Football game or stay home and make love to me?

Does it bother you that my ex's penis is bigger than yours?

Have you ever wanted to have a threesome?

Do you mind if my mother comes and stays with us for a month or so?

Practice, practice, practice. As Woody Allen said, I'm a good lover… "because I practice whenever I'm alone."

♂ ♂ ♂

In Recognition of Your Birthright,

For Your Courageous Commitment

To Our Cause and to Live Life as a

Member in Good Standing of

The All-American Man Club

For Demonstrating Your Manhood

Basically, for purchasing this Manual

You Are Hereby Awarded

1000 Points

On Your

All-American MAN CARD

Welcome to the Revolution

Membership Cards

Your membership into the All-American Man Club will be complete with an identification card that will enable you to trumpet your inclusion in our highly prestigious fraternity. Once again, the Brainiacs at R&D have devised this easy-to-follow explanation: Notice that your card has ten boxes on the front side. These are punishment boxes that another Member can mark to denote forfeiture of points for any egregious feminine behavior, membership rules violations, or blatant acts of servitude to women.

Should you, as a Member in Good Standing, witness any said breach of masculine behavior, or an act that qualifies on its own disgusting merits, you must for the good of all men, make one of the following notations on the offending Member's card: Draw one single diagonal line (/) in one box. This indicates a deduction of fifty (50) points. A second violation would result in another diagonal line forming an "X" in that box. This represents a total loss of one-hundred (100) points. At this point, the box can be punched out. If you have a hole-punch handy, you may skip the "X" stage and simply punch out the appropriate number of boxes to fit the violation. Example: A two-hundred, fifty point penalty would require either two "X's" and one diagonal line (/), or two punches and one diagonal line (/). In this manner, when all ten boxes have been either marked with an "X" or punched out, the violator's membership would be invalid and he would need to re-apply for a conditional membership. Note: before punching holes in any card, make sure you have retained the benefits information from the back side.

Wait, what the hell? Even we couldn't follow all that BS. Okay, what all that means is "X" or punch-out each box for every one-hundred points deducted; when the boxes are gone, he's gone. He loses his sack and suffers public humiliation and disdain. A fitting punishment. Confiscate and either destroy the card, or place it in a frame and display his shame for all the world to see, and notify Man Club Headquarters, at aamchq.com.

Conditional Membership Card: May be granted by applying via the website. This is a provisional membership with only five-hundred (500) points granted, Should the probationary Member lose those points, he will be condemned to a life of servitude, rife with ridicule and shame, bereft of man-sack including all accompanying rank and privilege.

♂ *The vanquished receive only suffering: torment, pain and humiliation. To the victors go the spoils.*

Reward System

While many of our Members have stated that possession of their own testicles and self-determination are reward enough, we do nonetheless have a reward system for the faithful compliance with the guiding principles of the All-American Man Club and our All-American Man Card. First, check the back of the card for benefits, deals, and special offers; we think you will be pleased, if not surprised. Note: Some cards were printed without these benefits but can be replaced for those with the benefits listed at no cost by notifying us at aamchq.com.

When meeting another Member in a social setting, the member with the fewest points must buy the first round of drinks. Honor System; Members don't cheat other Members! As a Member in

Good Standing, you are also entitled to numerous pleasant experiences that typically come with being associated with the club. We enjoy so many that we had to rate them in order of ascending pleasures. While not guaranteed, many Members routinely experience the following:

Scale of Pleasant Experiences

The, "It's so good you want it to last just a little bit longer, oh... please ...oh... Please!" good.

The, *"Yeah, baby, you know just what I like; right there, oh yes!"* good.

The, "Perfectly prepared, so tender it melts on your fork, 22-ounce King's cut prime rib, with salad, and a loaded baked potato" good.

The, "No, wait! Yiiieee! Stop! Don't touch that, it's too sensitive" good.

The, "My team just won the Super Bowl and I had them for $500 at 12/1!" good.

The, "I told her to shut the hell up or I'd send her to live with her mother!" good.

The, "She told you she thought it was time the two of you had a threesome with another woman!" good.

♂ ♂ ♂

♂ *Mankind has historically expanded its horizons. The world was populated by man's insatiable need for conquest and space; a man <u>needs</u> his own space, someplace to BE.*

CHAPTER TEN:
PLACES AND SPACES

As a single man, it is imperative that you protect your territory from any invader, especially domestic. Realize that at some point in your relationship, she will make her move, trying to control your space, ergo you, via the loving and innocent placing of some of her personal items into your home. Beware! You will be penalized for each of the following items you allow her to leave, uncontested, in your space at any time, in any amount, for any length of time, for any reason. To avoid incurring penalties for these violations, convince her to bring along an overnight bag. Skillfully let her know she's always welcome to stay overnight, but get cleaned up and take her $#!+ home in the morning!

List of problematic items: Toothbrush, feminine deodorant spray, feminine napkins, panty liners, favorite stuffed animal, tampons, any type of birth control device. "hot water bottle" or any product that references douching, furniture of any kind, electronic equipment, TV's, stereos, etc.

The only items you should allow her to bring into your home, besides take-out orders, are pain relievers. Allow both aspirin and non-aspirin products to provide a choice, but as an oh-so much more important strategy, to eliminate her possible complaint of having a "headache."

Remember the kind, caring, but firm approach here to avoid confronting the "you don't love me enough" trap. This is a thinly disguised ruse designed to lure you into commitment. The best defense here is to go with the "*I understand what you're saying, and I respect your feelings; so please respect mine. Right now, this is my place. Maybe, someday, who knows?*" Then when she focuses on the *maybe,* be ready with a distraction. Oh yeah, don't forget the chocolate.

Personal Space

In our never-ending search for all things male, we have discovered a few towns that sound as though they may be conducive to promoting the ideals of the All-American Man Club, and some places that probably are not. Of course, we had to find out for ourselves if these towns lived up to the promise of their monikers. For example, would you, as a Member in Good Standing, be comfortable visiting a town in Scotland named Dull? How about Boring, Oregon? There are even more menacing sounding city names, cities that sound so anti-male that we probably avoid visiting them. But there are some that are intriguing.

What's in a name? To find out, to grow the membership, to have a great time, and to get some time away from you know who, we developed the:

All-American Man Club World Tour 2012

Jan	Defiance, PA.
Feb	Intercourse, PA.
Mar	New Orleans, LA. - Mardi Gras
Apr	Kawasaki, Japan - Penis Festival
May	Dickensheet Junction, ID.
June	Bangor, MA.
July	New Beaver, PA.
Aug	Bush City, KS.
Sept	Manville, WY.
Oct	VEGAS BABY! Pimp & Ho Ball
Nov	Climax, NY.
Dec	Mayan Temple - If the World's Gonna End We're Gonna PARTY!
January '13 (CRAP!)	Back to work, pay off my credit cards

Places We Will Not Visit: Sassamansville, PA., Moody Beach, ME., Deadwood, CO., Fallen Timber, PA., Romance, AR., Blue Ball, PA., And of course, Boring, OR.

The Big Screen

If you think twenty-thousand dollars is a reasonable amount to pay for a 61" High Definition television with theater quality surround sound, but balk at forty-five bucks for a new comforter, you are our kind of guy. While women are indefatigable bargain hunters, with an innate ability to sniff out useless bargains, men instinctively understand the intrinsic value of the big screen on Super Bowl Sunday. That's the place Members want to be found, either there or staring up at women slithering seductively up or down, and hanging around on poles. That is the space we are meant to occupy.

Just try inviting half-a-dozen freeloaders over to watch the big game on a little 21-inch portable. Helpful hint: Anything with a handle on it doesn't belong in the living room. We suggest you try using the handle to carry it into the bedroom and connect it to DVD or Blu-Ray player. Note: If we have to explain the rest, just go ahead and send in your All-American Man Card, we'll gladly cancel your membership.

The reason for the disparity in the level of appreciation that men and women have for televisions is quite natural. It is genetic. We have a dominant and very important beauty appreciator gene. In women, it is either recessive or totally absent, except in lesbians, of course.

That's why most women constantly look in the mirror, they're not sure if they look good enough to compete with all the other women. Without the gene, they constantly compare themselves with each other in a vain attempt to reassure themselves that they can get laid by any man.

If women had the gene, they would have a greater appreciation for the beauty of the female form, and there would be more bi-sexual women. Like men and lesbians, who know the value of form and function, they would feel the blood-rush we feel when we see them in bikinis and thongs, or when we first lay eyes on that sweet 61" LCD.

♂ Let's be clear, take this to heart because you may not recognize the danger you are in. When women tell men that they are showing the world how masculine and confident men are by adopting some feminine behavior or look, they are unknowingly betraying their sinister plan, revealing they believe men are so dumb and gullible they'll do anything to get women into bed. The sad, unfortunate fact is, they are often right.

So please understand, there is nothing sexy, or confident, or remotely masculine about wearing a bun in your hair. There is no such thing as a "man-bun." Just because women cleverly labeled the horrendous coif, doesn't give the term any credibility. So males, lose the bun, you look ridiculous, and even if you are getting busy on a regular basis with a female who thinks, "It's cute and makes you look so masculine," it isn't, it doesn't; it makes you look feminine. So, lose it! That is unless that's the look you're going for. Then keep it, but read all about metrosexuals, and check your package at the door when you enter "her" place.

♂ An astute Member recently relayed the list of ten reasons why women don't want to have sex. We can think of at least ten good reasons why they do want to, but let's examine some of the items listed: being distracted, weight gain, lack of exercise, depression, relationship tension, you're uncomfortable and stressed out.

Well, of course they are! They've probably gained that weight *because* they're not exercising. They're probably sitting around being distracted by the little chocolate donuts in the cupboard and the 3000 calorie grande´ caramel macchiato into which they are dunking said little chocolate donuts. Big mystery here. Clue: When they partake in these health and fitness challenged activities, and end up fat and lazy, they are probably going to become uncomfortable and stressed out.

They also might not want to have sex, but you haven't lost any desire or testosterone, and you have needs—you *are* a man. So, show her some understanding and comfort her with this soothing message, "GOYA!" This stands for Get Off Your Ass. Put down the sweets and pick up some weights. In time, you'll be lifting your spirits along with those weights, and you may even get to be the lucky dog that finds a bone now and then. Men, here's another method for erasing those reasons not to have sex, eat healthy. Ladies, if any ignored the warnings and are reading this, encourage your man to eat well too. We have a T-Shirt that promotes both eating well and enjoying a healthy sex life. It reads, "Feed Your Member Tacos Tonight!"

♂ Another one of our Members shared this with HQ recently: Out the blue one morning over coffee, his wife asked him, "You know what I haven't used in a long time?"

Now, another man may have retorted with some crass statement about any number of things he wished his wife would use, but not our Member. He was tempted, but as an AAMC Member he knew how to treat women properly to ensure domestic tranquility and said, "No, tell me what you haven't used lately." Conflict avoided; chance of a mutually enjoyable domestic entanglement tonight, 100%.

♂ ♂ ♂

♂ *You don't have to be a Neanderthal to join the club, or even be the manliest man. However, you can't be the girliest guy and expect to be admitted. It's really all in the way you think...*

CHAPTER ELEVEN: RANDOM MANLY THOUGHTS

If you appear on CNN, as a noted expert in the field, discussing the manly, hot topic of Library Sciences, DO NOT send in your Man Card. Shred it, burn it, melt it in the microwave, whatever. Just make sure that whatever infected you cannot possibly be transmitted to any of us.

♂ A very misguided, but nonetheless pleasant woman contacted the All-American Man Club HQ recently with the following comment: Isn't it about time we redesigned our rockets? If we keep shooting these gigantic phallic symbols into space, no other beings will ever want to make contact with us. Who knows, maybe they think we're compensating for something?

Members believe that whenever you plan on meeting someone for the first time, you should always put your best foot forward. Want to make a good first impression? Show off your number one attribute. On this planet, nothing says who we are better than a 360 foot, fiery phallus with a secret military payload shooting up at you at 18,000 miles an hour.

♂ Researchers here at the Man Club HEAD-quarters have recently identified a direct, verifiable correlation between testosterone and channel-surfing.

What remains unclear at this time is if the testosterone creates the need for men to hold onto and lord over the remote control, or if the actual grasping of the living room scepter stimulates the production of the male hormone.

One theory postulates that both factors play equal roles, and that we are witnessing an evolutionary branching that could be of biblical proportions.

So, how does all this heavy science affect us? And what the hell did that last paragraph mean? We're not really sure, but it's definitely the last time we send the research department to Vegas for the weekend. And, we don't think they'll be doing any more writing anytime soon, not for this manual.

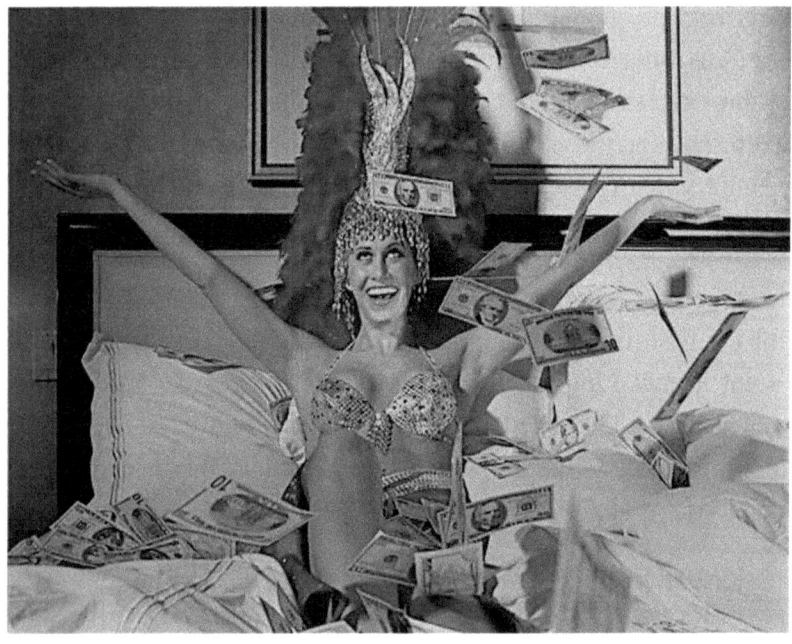

So, we'll try to explain why this is important information, without research, without the notes we needed that got lost, supposedly at the *Blue Man Group* show, but somehow ended up being held for ransom by a topless-showgirl dancer named Desiree', who sounded nice enough but apparently doesn't have a checking account since she demanded we pay in cash. Damn geeks, they owe us twelve-hundred bucks!

Back to science. Through scientific research, we gain the information, insight, and understanding that are the cornerstones of knowledge. As we know, knowledge is power. Aside from money, or being a woman with a vagina, knowledge is one of the most powerful forces in nature.

But money can get even the ugliest guys laid.

One of our Members once witnessed an old, hobo-looking derelict, had to be in his early seventies easy, talk a large young hooker into a back-door pop for a short roll of quarters. Yep, for ten bucks this dredge bends her over right in the Caesars Palace Sports Book next to the statue of Joe Louis.

But knowledge can be useful also. By understanding the scientific principles that lie at the core of specific behaviors, men can learn how to manipulate and control their relationships. Thus, they can finally gain an advantage in the never-ending struggle for dominion over the opposite sex.

Certainly, there is no question as to the effect of channel surfing, i.e., controlling the remote. Clearly this natural male behavior is representative of two critical factors in inter-gender relationships.

First, control is after all, control. The importance of gaining and maintaining control of a man's surroundings can never truly be overstated. Use any and every opportunity to win back whatever measure of control you can manage to wrest from their evil clutches.

Second, channel surfing demonstrates the male's natural proclivity for searching the other side of the fence for greener grass. Yeah, you know what we're talking about. Men are always looking, and women know it.

It is one of the amazing anomalies in the genetic makeup of men. We can be involved in a terrific relationship with a beautiful woman, she may even have money. It's smooth sailing but the Man in us is still searching the horizon for bigger sails.

Before you ask what's wrong with us, stop and think. Once again, we must! It's in our genes. But just think of what the effect is on our women when we jump with promiscuous disregard from channel to channel. It must unnerve even them beyond our wildest dreams. They hate it!

So, while we sit and change channels every forty seconds or so, we are sending a clear message to our mates: *We're perfectly happy to receive this broadcast for now, but if we get too bored or irritated, we won't hesitate to switch channels, and find one that we like just a little bit better. So, stay on your toes; or if you prefer, your knees, and keep us happy.*

Now if we could just get the mute button to work on them.

♂ One of our members reported a thoroughly disgusting display of non-manlike behavior recently. Seems he was in a doctor's office waiting room and decided to check out the latest issue of ESPN the Magazine. When he opened the manly magazine, he found, concealed inside, an issue of Women's Health! Not only was this … this person guilty of reading a fem-mag, he wasn't even man enough to read it openly and with emboldened confidence proclaim, *I'm reading this, what's it to you?* Hope he was in there for a sex change operation.

♂ We are a clever and imaginative bunch. We give great names to the everyday products we use. We recognize the trend as clever advertising, shrewd market analysis, and opportunistic product placement. Sometimes it's braggadocio, often it's only wishful thinking, but it's almost always a metaphor that symbolizes our fondness of, devotion to, and obsession with sex.

Take for example, the line of clubs made by golf club manufacturer Adams Golf, known as *The Tight Lies.* Question: Didn't Adam have the tightest lie of all time? Don't we all yearn for a tight lie just one more time? How long has it been? We wonder if those thoughts occurred to the folks at Adams Golf when they named the clubs, or if this is just another case of happy providence.

Another example is in the great game of football. There are Tight Ends, who get their hands on the ball only a few times compared to the Wide Receivers. Is it a coincidence that most Wide Receivers can't even run down the field without flapping their lips?

♂ **Here's something to think about: Famous Women?**

Joan of Arc - Burned at the Stake for heresy.

Lizzie Borden - Hacked up her parents with an axe.

Martha Stewart - Convict.

Lorena Bobbitt - Whacked off J. Wayne's little member, and not in the good way.

Eve - the Mother of All Evil.

Pandora - Look at what happened when she opened her box.

Marie Antoinette - Couldn't keep her mouth shut, lost her head.

Martha Burk - Who? Oh yeah, a few years ago she paid to bus in women from an all-girl college to protest Augusta National's *"no women members"* rule at the Master's Championship. Had more press corps and Elvis impersonators than protesters and set their movement back ten years. From those of us at The All-American Man Club, a heartfelt THANK YOU goes out to this failed crusader! Interesting note: They tried again in 2012 claiming that the CEO of one of the tournament's major sponsors was a female and her predecessors—all men--had been accepted as members. The result: Denied again! Way to go Augusta!

Update: Finally happened, even the best party has to end. Took a CEO with a boatload of money; at least they "put her on a leash." But it wasn't Martha's pressure that opened the door, it was good old fashioned cash, the kind with the picture of a *Man* on the front.

♂ *The Cathouse Series* on cable TV was one of our favorite diversions from the daily grind that is: Reclaiming Our Manhood. We love to watch as Ho's and Johns hook up to transmit bodily fluids, diseases, and currency. It's a great show, and it is filmed not far from the All-American Man Club HEADquarters. In fact, now that we think of it, our R&D guys seemed to spend a great deal of time there conducting research…

However, one episode aired featured a young male whose girlfriend had paid to send him to the ranch to learn how to be "dominant." No, really! Honest! Wait though, it gets more bizarre.

During his "party" with his hand-selected date, the viewing public, which was perhaps about 10 million guys, learned that this hapless sap couldn't even flog his own log, let alone flog the girl *he* chose. But wait! Here comes the disgusting part.

Right there on national cable, the party provider decides that this tool is too much of a wussy to ever pull off being dominant, and she *tells him*, in front of everybody! Then she turns the tables on him and makes *him* become submissive! If it wasn't for the generous gratuitous nudity, we would have switched the channel to MXC.

Chalk up another convert. They own him now. There is nothing anyone can do. It's so sad; he had his whole life in front of him, so young …

We can only say that if it was one of our Members, we would impose an immediate exile up some river somewhere where men couldn't see him and wouldn't be reminded of our shame.

♂ Let's be clear, take this to heart because you may not recognize the danger you are in. When women tell men that they are showing the world how masculine and confident men are by adopting some feminine behavior or look, they are unknowingly betraying their sinister plan, revealing they believe men are so dumb and gullible they'll do anything to get women into bed. The sad, unfortunate fact is, they are often right.

So please understand, there is nothing sexy, or confident, or remotely masculine about wearing a bun in your hair. There is no such thing as a "man-bun." Just because women cleverly labeled the horrendous coif, doesn't give the term any credibility. So males, lose the bun, you look ridiculous, and even if you are getting busy on a regular basis with a female who thinks, "It's cute and makes you look so masculine," it isn't, it doesn't; it makes you look feminine. So, lose it! That is unless that's the look you're going for. Then keep it, but read all about metrosexuals, and check your package at the door when you enter "her" place.

Don't forget The Plan concocted by women to rid the world of man's rightful dominion over women. The Plan includes the complete subjugation of men, and calls for the total destruction of the gender. They'll get in your head to accomplish it.

♂ We've heard of a tiny tribe, known as the Mhobun, hundreds of miles inland somewhere in a remote corner of the Amazon jungle. They are a notoriously feminine bunch of males who live under the subjugation of their women, who "allow" their males to fish all day in the Cha′Pu Sea. This sounds like a perfect place for our nutless friend. He should be exiled to live forever among the Mhobun. By the way, their name actually means many, or several, and is pronounced with a soft but longer "m." The name of the region is always included, and when you say it in their native speech it sort of runs together. It comes out sounding like this: mmm-hobunchapuseas.

♂ *A good craftsman never blames his tools. The right tool in the hands of a skilled craftsman is a beautiful thing to watch.*

Women and Sex Are Like Power Tools

Work Area: Keep your work area free of debris and obstacles. Tools not in use should be kept free of dirt and dust. Properly clean your tool before use. A dirty tool can cause any number of health issues.

Inspect Tools: Check for cracks, damage or other problems. Damaged tools can cause injury, such as loose parts flying off and hitting someone. Check for nicks and other damage. Repair or throw away tools that are defective.

Proper Clothing: Properly strap down any moving parts. Wear eye goggles or safety glasses whenever working with potentially dangerous tools. Use earplugs to protect hearing and maintain sanity. Hard hats and sturdy gloves should always be worn during heavy jobs. Long pants protect against flying debris, but can be removed quickly when opportunities present themselves. In extreme cases, a Haz-Mat suit is recommended.

Correct Tools: Use the right tools for the job you are doing. Many injuries occur when using the wrong tool for a project. Many body parts get cut from scraping against an object because the wrong tool caused slippage. Use, purchase or borrow the right tools for each job. If you don't have the right tool, wait on the project until you do.

Properly Store Tools: When not in use, tools can easily fall into the wrong hands. Put tools away in a safe place when the work is complete. Make sure tools are unplugged and put back in their containers.

Proper Lighting: Ensure that the area where you are working has the proper mood lighting. Add spice and variety by working outdoors during the day. Indoors, work in the best light or bring extra lighting into the area if necessary. Injuries often occur in areas with poor lighting.

Focus: Always be mindful when using. Tools do not think. They do not know the difference between their intended use, and whatever flesh you might absent-mindedly place in their way. Do not distract a person who is using a tool, and try to limit the chances of being distracted when you are using your tool.

♂ *Some women find us vulgar, others find us at night.*
If we find the right women, things will work out all right.

CHAPTER TWELVE:
FINDING THE RIGHT WOMAN

This is the one life quest in which you must be successful. So, you think it may be time to settle down. You are satisfied with the oats you've sown, and understand your lifestyle will forever be changed. No longer will you be free to order pizza and wings, grab a cold beer out of the fridge, and plant your carcass in front of the big screen all day Sunday. You're okay with that because you know you won't have to get the beer yourself, she can bring it to you.

Here's a slap in the face wake-up for you. The concepts of True Love, of There Is Someone for Everyone, and of Finding Your Soul Mate are archaic, romanticized, and tragically droll. These inept "wish-for" methods of selecting the right person for you and of trusting fate to deliver your one special match made in heaven have been carefully crafted in romantic drivel. We refuse to use the terms novels and movies use to confuse, confound and control you. That is part of their Plan, not ours. Their hope is you will regard the first woman who, for some unknown reason, is nice to you as the one for whom you have been searching. Don't buy into this.

We have a better system.

Since you've decided to start looking around for that special someone to wait on you hand and foot, for the rest of your life, or until you get tired of her crap, we decided to give you some guidelines to make sure your selection is right for the man you are. We consulted our research department and asked them to supply some ideas for helping you along on your soggy path of destruction. When they sobered up, they came up with some pretty interesting points of view.

It used to be asked of nubile, young women, by frustrated old women who never experienced the ecstasy of a man-induced orgasm, "Why should he buy the cow, when he gets the milk for free?"

This was their way of steering young virgins away from the evils of pre-marital sex, and thereby ensuring the ability of the chaste to land a good man. This was prior to the sexual revolution. Now, finding a virgin bride is about as likely as Martha Burk being the Guestess of Honor at the Champions Dinner at the Masters.

But you can still find the right mate for you. Our R&D Department suggests that you employ the most modern problem-solving device to assist you in one of the oldest quests a man can undertake. Yes, of course, use the Internet! Google it! Although they are big time geeks, our R&D nerds may be on to something. They seem to think that searching for a mate is a lot like buying a car.

On UsedWives&Girlfriends.suk, you may be able to select the model that's just right for you and fits your budget. You can look up thousands of possible models and find their history, driving record, their mileage, how many previous owners, and any wrecks they've had.

Now be careful, avoid the showroom floor models. They're

usually expensive and high-maintenance. Look for more than just low rates and easy financing, and don't fall in love with the first one you drive. Test-drive several models before you make the ultimate decision. And of course, check the trunk space.

Don't worry if you are new in town, have bad credit, bankruptcy, or even a divorce. You can still drive off the lot with one today; it just might not be the model you really wanted. Keep in mind that the more you have up front to put down, the less you'll pay over time.

Just be thankful you're driving.

So, whether you're looking for a sporty little two-seater with racing stripes and great curves, or a dependable, low-mileage, carry the kids around wagon, check the web site before you make a commitment. Remember: You'll be riding with every owner that's ever driven her.

♂ *Learn to read women, it will give you a tremendous advantage in whatever arena you find yourself competing. For example, did you know that in a recent study of women's brain wave activity, mentioning chocolate references elicited the same responses as the words diamonds and commitment? Also, there were no responses to football, baseball, art and literature, but test subjects became flushed, highly responsive, had dilated pupils, and were virtually aroused at "Ghirardelli."*

Dating

Some guys have the knack, no trouble whatsoever making and successfully consummating the date. To be real, at the end of the night this is the ultimate goal. Other guys just seem to fall a little short when it comes to engaging the opposite sex. And by that we mean the social intercourse exchanges, not the personal interchange of bodily fluids type.

For some reason, which we cannot fathom, some guys get nervous, tongue-tied, and sweat profusely in social situations involving the possibility of having sex with a random stranger instead of their usual blow-up doll. Members don't get it. What is there to be afraid of, to cower away from clearly demonstrating your lack of self-confidence?

Guys, it's only women! Remember, they want exactly what you want, good sex! What could be easier? So, get out there and beat the bushes, it's much more fulfilling than beating your own member.

Here are some quick thoughts, easy advice for those of you who are novice consummators:

Don't:

Flirt with the waitress. Seems like common sense, but some guys just don't know how to keep it in their pants. Don't be that guy. A bird in the hand is worth two in the bush. If you break this rule and mac up your server, then the only bush your hand will be in will be your own.

Criticize what your date orders, how much food she eats or leaves and don't eat half your date's meal. Even if she isn't hungry, or pretending not to be, restrict all extemporaneous eating urges for when you get her to the motel.

Argue with the server. This move is certain date-death. You

might think you're showing her who's the boss, but you can forget about showing her who's her daddy!

Go anywhere near anyplace with a crown, an arch, a bell or a star on the sign. Really? Looking for an explanation here? Look, we have nothing against any of these types of establishments, but if you don't take her to a nice sit-down restaurant, you won't be holding anything against her, ever. See what we did there?

Complain about the prices. The definition of cheap: miserable, lonely, miser, tightwad, a lonely masturbator.

Scope any other chicks! Women possess an incredibly sensitive, highly developed, innate sense that detects when you are looking at other women. They know! See: Flirt with, above.

Order for her, unless she requests it. Show her some respect. You already know she craves power, let her have her way now and have your way with her later.

Order anything you don't recognize. Only a simp would risk accidentally ordering some slimy, foul-smelling, unknown entrée that may have to be spit out. What kind of message do you think THAT will send to her. Stay away from making any spit or swallow decisions, that's her territory.

Talk more than you listen. Shut the front door! It's not about getting your ego stroked; that isn't the part you should worry about stroking.

Make sure you get the receipt for a tax write-off. Actually, if you're prone to this type of thinking, you probably aren't going out on a lot of dates anyway, are you? Admit it, c'mon.

Do:

Expect a little something. You know, for the effort.

Hey, if you paid for the meal, and showed her a good time, you deserve… well… Okay, so hope for it, but don't think you're entitled. There is a tremendous amount of lip service about honesty in relationships. If you are not looking for a permanent shackle, then be man enough to let her know. Perhaps she will appreciate your honesty in knowing that you are not looking for any long-term commitments at this time. Perhaps you can get a little service of your own? Who knows, maybe you are looking for someone long-term. We don't know why, but it happens.

If all goes well, and that is a relative term, then your relationship has the potential to move from level to level with increasing commitment. If you do want a more permanent relationship, beware! There are fem-planned pitfalls around every mound, hidden traps behind every bush.

One of those traps can be anticipated and you can deploy a pre-emptive strike to maintain control. There is a new diabolical tactic emerging from the plotters at the evil axis of women.

Relationship Agreements

Lately there has been a disturbing trend; women seeking not only pre-nuptial agreements, but relationship agreements as well. Evidently, items such as whose families will visit and/or be visited, how your finances will be divided and controlled, and the number of times per week that you will be having sex are now negotiable items to be included in these thinly disguised power-play instruments of law.

Members instinctively understand from their genetic link to football that the best defense is a strong offense. Not just another bad cliché. Take action! Beat her to the master control station with your own version of the relationship agreement. Design whatever stipulations you feel are necessary, but as in any battle, strike first, strike hard! To assist you getting the ball rolling, here's a sample of a club approved agreement:

The All-American Man Club Relationship Agreement

Let it be known to all that the parties signed below have entered into this agreement willingly and without threat or coercion. This document defines the parameters of said parties' roles in this relationship and is intended to serve as an instrument of law. This agreement is a binding contract between two consenting adults and becomes effective immediately upon receipt of signatures.

Let it further be known and understood that I, _____, the Man in this relationship will do my best to keep you happy if doing so does not interfere with my normal routine and/or my personal pursuits of happiness, or jeopardize my masculinity in any way, shape or form.

Further, we are together now because you were attracted to me when we met. If not, all those nasty little feel-good things we do, and of which you have become quite fond, would never have happened. Since you continue to beg for more and more, I must surmise that your initial attraction to me, however shallow it was, must surely have grown into deep affection. Over time you have gotten to know the real me and our relationship has progressed to the point that we are contemplating this serious step in our lives. In other words, you like what you see, and what you see is what you get. Therefore, you will not waste any time or effort trying to change me, because I like me just the way I am and evidently, so do you. Therefore, as we move forward you agree to the following terms and conditions:

By signing below, I _____, the little woman, the supportive, faithful and understanding weaker member of the team, being of sound mind and smokin' hot body do hereby understand and agree that, _____ is who he is and will continue to be so without interference or meddling from me. I agree to willingly and joyfully accept that he:

Stares at beautiful women, scratches his genitals in public, drinks beer whenever and wherever possible, goes hunting, fishing/camping when it pleases him, plays poker with his buddies one night a week, wants sex all the time, regularly attends collegiate and/or professional sporting events, hits nudie bars whenever necessary, owns, operates and refuses to sell a hot car that will attract women, often has biological urges and/or functions that need to be addressed, leaves way too big a tip for flirty waitresses, is never polite to my relatives, has a sordid, checkered past that he brags about with his pals, has no feminine side to explore, will not sit and watch chick flicks or wear matching outfits, watches sports on TV incessantly—and doesn't care that he doesn't know what incessantly means, does not go shopping at the mall on Sundays, has a terrible memory for birthdays and anniversaries, has equal parts imagination and libido--especially regarding three-ways, absolutely refuses to be *whipped*, and he participates in other manly pursuits. I understand that these are what makes him a Man. He is All Man and he is My Man! So, God love him for the Man he is because

I hereby agree to!

Signed, the little woman,

_____Date_____

Be it also known that I _____ the Man and rightfully dominant partner, do hereby agree to do as much as any man can to try to understand those few times when she fails to abide by this agreement. I'm good with the rest of it.

Signed, the lord of the manor,

_____Date_____

♂ ♂ ♂

♂ *Sometimes, when women get together and rail against the machine that is man, they can be very comical. Not that they are trying to make us laugh, that's just the inevitable result.*

CHAPTER THIRTEEN:
THEY ARE JUST SO CUTE…

We are often quite amused at some of the cute little notions they have in their pretty little heads following a Women's [anything] meeting or rally. They get all fired-up and want to go out and change the world! Or, at least find another method of eviscerating men. Inevitably, feminist rhetoric spews forth steadily, with predictable outcome. Members are warned to be aware of the tell-tale signs including, evisceration of men, attempts to overturn the natural order, and exaggerated, wholly outlandish claims. Here are some of our favorites:

If women ran the world there would be no war.

Oh, really? Tell that to the people in the Falkland Islands. When they tried to assert their independence, what did Maggie T, the Fem PM do? She sent warships, planes and troops to crush the rebellion. You think Carrie was pissed off? Next to Maggie T, Carrie looked like she had a mild case of PMS!

Or, shall we consider Queen Mary I, appropriately nicknamed Bloody Mary, who had huge numbers of Protestants murdered in England. Hundreds of thousands more fled her reign of terror that lasted until her death in 1558.

If women were in charge, the world would run more

smoothly and efficiently.

Oh, really? How about the evil brought about by Biljana Plavšic´ in Bosnia-Herzegovina, the former president of Republic Srpska, whose comments that "ethnic cleansing" was a "good thing" and that six million Serbs had to die, rallied her republic to commit the Serbian genocides of the1990's.

Besides, would we honestly be comfortable with entrusting the efficiency of an entire planet to people who cannot get off the cell phone while they put on their make-up and fly maniacally down the highway, thirty miles over the speed limit in an SUV that is twice as big as they can handle? AND, these are the same people that have absolutely no concept of time or measurement? Proof? Ever see a woman who was on time and could show you the exact and correct length of eight inches? Plus, our cracked research troops theorize that it was in fact, a woman who was responsible for the measurements during the construction of the Tower of Pisa. Look at what happened there. Of course, that part is just a theory.

All men ever think about is sex.

Oh, rea... Well…that is pretty much true. But it's not completely accurate. We do need twenty minutes of rest and recovery from time to time, and what about sports? Members don't think, *"That was the greatest catch I've ever seen. I need to get laid now!"* Besides, we may think about sex most of the time, but a lot of women sure are glad we do.

God is A Woman?

We are sometimes amazed by some of the theories women try to pass as fact. If not for the fact that they somehow believe their tripe and expect us to believe it is our duty to follow along, their rants would be hilarious.

Take for example the notion they espouse that GOD is a woman. Stop laughing, remember, they take themselves very seriously, and they are teaching this to your daughters. Yeah, yeah, we know, the Bible was written by men, yadda, yadda. The best attack we've found for combating this ludicrous idea is to list examples that show that if God were a woman, these things simply would not, could not possibly be true. So, here is the indisputable list:

Menstruation: The curse, as it known to those who are afflicted by its monthly ravages. If that is not enough, think: tampons, cramps, douches, feminine deodorant sprays, bloating, PMS. There are no products specifically made for men requiring we spray anything up any of our crevasses.

Childbirth: Perhaps the most grueling, painful feat of endurance ever devised. And for what? To provide *us* with offspring; heirs to the throne. Who got handed this little chore?

Orgasms and Ejaculations: Which one is easier to achieve? Who has to fake them? Do they ever roll over and go to sleep before *you* get yours? This gift *must* have been bestowed by a male deity.

Breasts: Everybody should stop pretending that we don't judge women by the size, shape, and potential comfort level of their bulbous mammary glands. The more bulbous the better. You know it, they know it, we all do it. Some will counter that the same is true for men and the size of their man-candles. Ah, but where are the respective parts located? Ours are cleverly situated so as to be easily concealed, prolonging and adding to the mystery of the big reveal, but the mamms are right out there for everyone to see, and judge. What gender do you think designed that arrangement?

Life Expectancy: If God were a woman, men would outlive women, thereby increasing the length of time men would have to suffer on this planet, and the enjoyment women would derive from that suffering as they sat in heaven eating chocolates without gaining any weight.

The Garden of Eden: No way a female deity lets women take the blame for that ejection. We were supposed to occupy that real estate for countless generations. So, who is responsible for the first premature ejection? Hint: It wasn't Adam, you know, the man.

Basketball: Would be played in the nude in front of sell-out crowds of women and gay guys. Dribbling would take on a whole new meaning. The arena vendors would all be selling bonbons and wine coolers.

Weights and Measurements: How many bulimic men do you know? How many women are there that know the true length of a foot-long sub sandwich? How many women know the real size of their dresses or their shoes? Well, most do, but won't admit it.

Football: While there are many, many women who enjoy football, there are very few men who enjoy shopping, quilting bees, and soap operas. Those that do are of questionable gender.

Besides, HE must be a MAN; if not, there wouldn't even be any foot… Wait, we've already covered this, but it *is* important. There *is* football. That should be proof enough.

College Recruiting: Vassar and other male-gender-challenged colleges do not have sex parties to recruit top high school prospects for their field-hockey teams, at least none of which we are aware. But, some men's college teams have done it…

Recent DNA testing of some recovered remains of the Anasazi, ancient inhabitants of Chaco Canyon in New Mexico, showed they were a people governed by a succession of one family, with ruling power handed down from mother to daughter for several generations. For some unknown reason, all the people left 3000 years ago and never returned. All that remains are ruins. If God were a woman, wouldn't they still be there, going strong and still subjugating men?

But they aren't there. Much like a frat house in July, nothing but dust, dirt, and the sporadic DNA sample is left for archaeologists to dig through.

There you have it. This certainly isn't an all-inclusive list. There are undoubtedly countless more examples. For those of you who continue to have trouble convincing her, let her mull over this last little tidbit; if God were a woman, men's tongues would hang below our chins, and we would be able to hold our breath for thirty minutes.

♂ *Little Known Fact: There is no such thing as vagina envy.*

Our Vaunted Research and Development Department

Although they don't have the same measurable attributes with which women are blessed, our R&D department nerds are cute in their own peculiar ways. We've kidded and cajoled, and have given our loveable geeks a spot of bad press here and there, but we need to show them our appreciation, acknowledge them for all their hard work, the long hours of diligent research, and their innate ability to view problems from so many different perspectives.

Without them, this manual would not have been, well, what it is. We're not pointing fingers either. A little history:

It began, as most sociological studies begin, inauspiciously as an off-the-cuff discussion that grew into a movement. The major topics were women, relationships between men and women, and the state of masculinity in our culture. It quickly developed into a think tank, generating theories, postulations, and socio-political constructs more rapidly than the participants could track.

The group decided that the subject needed a formal treatise, and that a concrete body of knowledge needed to be presented to the world. Thus, the research department formed and the foundation laid for the counter revolution.

Based in a small, two-room adobe in New Mexico, not far from Los Alamos in the late 1990's, the three original founding members of the All-American Man Club dove headfirst into the project at hand. What were their qualifications? Did they have advanced degrees? Education? Who needs it? One of them had been married once and divorced. One of them was in his second marriage, and it was going well, and their designated leader—a man with stone gonads--had been married three times. Don't talk of education, they had experience! The greatest teacher of all!

Admittedly, not all the theories and conclusions are based on 100% verifiable science. But we know scientists have been disseminating misinformation for centuries. Our theory is that the men of the day knew the truth, but embarked on a campaign of fake news to maintain the status quo of the relationships between men and women. By keeping the truth from women, men hoped to delay the eventual women's revolution and keep their women safely tucked away at home, segregated from would-be defilers for as lengthy a time as humanly possible.

It's just a theory. We could be wrong, but we still know an awful lot of guys who try to keep their women at home and cover up what they've done by making $#!+ up.

When we started this sack-saving-endeavor, we weren't lying or deflecting, we weren't holding back the truth, we intended to expose it. We were doing what men do on Sundays in the fall. We had the Forty-Niners vs. Raiders game on TV and money on the outcome. The pizza guy had just delivered our hot pie, the beer was ice-cold, and we were watching football and talking women. We were MEN conducting research! This manual is the result. Wait, did I say we…I meant them, yeah, those…those um… other researcher guys. Yeah, not me.

♂ *Civilized society demands cooperation of the masses. There are always consequences for non-compliance.*

CHAPTER FOURTEEN:
PENALTIES FOR NON-MASCULINE BEHAVIOR

As previously explained, you have been awarded, by the nature of your birth and your commitment to this cause, a total of 1000 points on your All-American Man Card. These points are "on loan" and can be rescinded at any time. But do not fear, no one will come and "bobbitize" your manhood for acting in a manner that promotes male/female hybridization.

By following the membership guidelines, and adhering to a masculine way of life, your points, your card, and your nads will all be safe. However, failure to act in a masculine manner does have consequences. Feminine acts can result in disciplinary action from deduction of points, up to and including separation from the club, and termination of your privileges, not to mention your sex life, your man-freedom, and your aforementioned nads.

The following scenarios are provided as a guide to assist you in navigating the treacherous waters known to all members as *relationships,* the kind that require no signed agreements.

Congratulations! You are booked to appear on a popular television show. Not only will you get paid good money for showing up, but you'll get to meet the host in person! And, you didn't even know your wife knew the producer of the Steve Wilkos Show. We hope your Mother-in-Law wasn't invited on the show with you. If you escape with a shred of dignity, you will be assessed only 100 points. Naturally, the only way to do this is to kick the living crap out of the other guy they bring on to embarrass you. So, in your case you'll probably get a hefty 200-point deduction.

You are well known for screaming at your kid's youth athletic league coach--in any sport--for the "mishandling" of your child prodigy. Chances are that your kid is more mature than you. This isn't the Kid Card, or Juvenile Card, it is the All-American *Man Card*. Time to grow up and LET THE KIDS PLAY! If youth sports are that serious to you, give your Membership Card to your mommy until you grow up. Have some cookies and milk, deduct 500 points, and go take a nap.

She calls a popular local morning radio show and names you as her "Man on a Leash." Deduct 300 points, and another 100 if you don't get her either under control or out the door.

More than half of your bathroom counter space is cluttered with curling irons, soaps, oils, brushes, lotions and potions designed to make her think she looks better than she does. Single guys lose 10 points for every item and see: Personal Space. Married guys receive an automatic 200-point deduction. Don't try to deny it, you know her stuff is there taking up well over half the counter and shelves.

You walk into a major strip casino in Las Vegas and proclaim to your friends, "I'll lay you even money that I can get us a table at Bradley Ogden's." Please, whatever you do in life, don't ever say anything this stupid. *Laying* odds on let's say a two-to-one bet means that if you win you will get *one* dollar for every *two* dollars that you bet. When you lay the odds, you get the smaller number. So, if you lay $200, you can win $100. *Taking* the odds is the exact opposite; you would bet $100 to win $200. You cannot lay even money! We wouldn't be surprised if the only thing *you could lay* came equipped with a juicy-red, little, round mouth and an inflation nozzle! You will forfeit 300 points for this ignorance and forfeit any chance of ever being cool.

Quick Quiz: What two NFL teams always play on Thanksgiving Day? Add 50 points for each right answer; deduct 100 points for each wrong answer. Take off another 100 if you whined about the penalty--you should have known the answer.

At a cocktail party, in the company of your friends and co-workers, she loudly states that you are nowhere near brave enough to run with the bulls in Pamplona. And, even if you were, you would never survive. Lose 200 points for Lack of Spousal/Significant Other Control. Here's a chance for some positive points; gain 500 points if you kick the impudent wench to the curb!

Since you've been running late all day, you cut short your workout to get home in time to watch reruns of the unfathomably popular TV show, *"Will and Grace."* Deduct 100 points for this show and/or any of the following: "The Good_Wife," "Glee," "Parenthood," or any other thinly-disguised prime-time soap opera.

Your recent visit to the proctologist revealed that you have a swollen prostate. The good news is that it's just temporary, you'll be fine. The bad news is that you really enjoyed the examination. Surrender one-half of your points, and become a Metrosexual.

She books a trip to Pamplona, Spain to run with the bulls, for her. She's arranged for you to spend a week at a mountain retreat getting in touch with your feminine side. If you accept these arrangements, just burn your membership card.

If you are overly concerned about what your male coworkers are wearing to the office, it may be time to get off the estrogen therapy. The guys probably aren't joking when they ask, "Can you GET any more feminine?" Helpful Hint: Take a close look at yourself, see if you're developing breasts. Deduct 300 points.

You may have more serious issues than we can address here if you have you ever asked your work buddies if they thought you had attractive legs, then defended yourself by saying, "Hey, you've seen my legs, don't you think they're sexy?" Minus 400 points, and we have our eye on you. No, not on your legs.

If you memorized exactly what tampons and panty liners to buy and actually purchase them, alone, on a regular basis, you are either very self-confident, or hopelessly whipped. We'll reserve the right to adjust your points when we see you at the annual convention. But just a word to the wise, don't memorize details about what the rest of us don't even want to hear, or even think about! Let her buy her own feminine hygiene products, go hunt something.

You let her name your penis. Big mistake; we hope for your sake that it isn't a small mistake. Anytime something is named, there is an establishment of implied ownership. You'll be penalized for your loss of control, and take an additional hit if she names it anything really cutesy or wimpy or anything femmed-out. Names like Mr. Blinky, Little Guy, Tiny Tim, My Little…anything, and Poke-ME-Man are totally unacceptable.

You can reduce the penalty though if she named it something that reflects the man you are. Names like The Quakemaker, My Fiend Flicka, G.W. Bushbuster, or anything to do with missiles and rockets will lessen the severity of your punishment. Minus 300 points for any named member, especially if it's femmed-out; however, add 100 bonus points for an appropriately named Manlius Erecticus.

A good friend is getting married and you are invited to his bachelor party. She throws a fit because she suspects that there may be strippers there conducting a little hookeration on the side. You're almost positive hookers doing that thing they do is exactly why you want to go in the first place, but she forbids your participation in this natural manly rite of passing. You have some critical choices to make:

One: Respect her feelings and wishes. You understand that she feels threatened and vulnerable, so you choose not to go. **Two:** Let her know you realize how afraid she is, but you can be trusted. Tell her your love for her will make you immune to even the most wicked temptations. She cries and you decide it's best that you stay at home.

Choosing either of these options will no doubt solidify your relationship with your soon to be anointed Queen of the Manor. Guess we won't be seeing you at the convention in Vegas this year, eh? That's okay, you might want to spend some time saying goodbye to your gonads; you won't need them, but you might get occasional visitation privileges. Minus 500 points.

There are two other choices:

Three: Realize that her response is merely just another power play craftily designed and carried out to keep you under the whip. Just tell her she needs to grow out of it and start trusting you. Grab some singles and hit the door. **Four:** Offer to drop her off at her mother's, or the bus station, or anywhere else that's on the way. Let her know that her behavior is totally unacceptable, meaning you're not putting up with her $#!+ any longer, and you have no intention of missing this party!

Plus 200 for option three; 500 for option four. These are the kind of responses that will get a man the respect he deserves! The kind that will earn him the admiration of his fellow All-American Man Club conventioneers! We'll reserve a special table and a spot for you at the gentlemen's club, close to the pole! Bring plenty of singles.

♂♂♂

GLOSSARY

Bobbitize: The shameful, horrendous act of physically and painfully removing any genitalia from a male, especially with the aid of a bladed weapon of devastation, which effectively renders said male impotent or otherwise unable to fulfil the basic functions, duties and responsibilities of his gender.

Coronal Mass Ejection: To some nerds this could have something to do with solar flares, but the AAMC Member knows that this describes that magical moment of sweet release, just before you roll over and go to sleep.

Critical Mass: Has absolutely nothing to do with nuclear energy. This is the point at which a man's sexual frustration reaches its maximum sustainable level. Any additional sensual stress will cause a cataclysmic meltdown resulting in definitive sexual acts. In this case, she needs to know--something's getting the pole tonight!

Bitchland: That place she travels to monthly during her cycle, also known as The Curse. Marked by incessant whining, moaning and verbal harassment of innocent males. Recognizable by three intertwining phases: Pre: The first week, here we go again. Where can I hide? Mid: This dangerous phase, a.k.a. the river phase. Might as well hang out at a nudie bar this week. And Post: the depression phase, wherein nothing you do is right, you can't make her happy, and everything is your fault! Due to these three phases, the total number of peaceful days you can expect in each 28-30-day cycle is perhaps a week, maybe ten days, tops.

Eunuchville: The deplorable and depraved state in which males live as a result of either: being passive, sensitive, and acting in a feminine manner or, lacking the requisite masculine traits necessary to maintain control and/or possession of one's testicles, a.k.a. nutless subservience. See: Grow a pair.

Expandamamms: The pinnacle of feminine charms and attributes. The natural result of women knowing they need to look their best to attract a mate. Wrongfully categorized as less appealing than real by some (Not Us) but they do need to be smaller than watermelons.

Grammamamms: The unfortunate result of time and gravity on the female breast. Causes drooping and flat appearance, and can be viewed by some as unflattering. However, many older Members find them quite titillating.

Grow a pair: The usual and natural response by most people to any male who lacks the gonadal fortitude to accept the normal responsibilities and perform the duties that any reasonable person would typically associate with being a man. Failure is tantamount to allowing your man-package to be kicked around like a hacky-sack.

Hookeration: The willful conducting of the oldest profession: supplying that for which a huge demand exists, and helping society maintain a calm and even temperament at the direct expense of only the person purchasing said service. A staple component of any memorable bachelor or bachelorette party, certain group celebrations, and individual mood stabilizers; a worldwide service commodity.

Lusciomamms: The perfectly sized, perfectly formed, and

perfectly luscious female breast expandamamms.

Outsourcing: Finding and utilizing an entity that lies beyond your immediate organizational structure that can, either by expertise, expedience, or cost effectiveness, better perform vital functions to increase your productivity, morale, and long term stability; i.e. getting some strange.

Pussoppression: The willful and wanton act of controlling male behavior by the implied, threatened, or actual withholding of sexual favors. The fiendish use of a woman's God-given gifts to subvert the natural order and subjugate men.

Viagravate: The act of fully and completely over-satisfying the needs and expectations of your lover to the point of exhaustion and pain via the use of any male enhancement product.

Viagravation: You're ready for another trip to O-ville, but she says all of her O-rifices are too raw and tender.

Viagravated: That moment when she finally says, "Get your ass off me! If you're still not done, go find the cat!"

Womanessence: That which makes women…women. The true nature of what is desirable to men. Nature's gift. The most delightful, pleasant, and compelling attributes in the known universe. Historically put to use servicing mankind, but in the wrong hands, can be used to promote evil.

♂ *"Governments are instituted among Men, deriving their just powers from the consent of the governed."*

Join the Get Your Sack Back Pack!

Now is the time for all good Men to reclaim our birthright as the dominant gender of this species! We need to remain vigilant against their evil plan of world domination. We need to band together as brothers to save Man-Sacks everywhere! The time for action is upon us. Don't be misled by their ample gifts, don't be confused by their manipulative power plays and empty promises. Get your sack back, or help save another brother's. Remember the All-American Man Club principles; they can guide you in times of need. We'll be here if you need us. You'll recognize us with ease; we'll be the guys with smiles on our faces, standing stiff, erect, confident and proud in the middle of the room. Join us, brother.

Unicus Dominus - Vir

One Ruler - Man!

♂ ♂ ♂

ABOUT THE AUTHORS:

Forrest Nelson is an author living in Spokane, Washington with his wife, two dogs, one cat, and none of them overly fond of him. After retiring from over thirty years in the casino surveillance/security field, Forrest now devotes much of his time to studying current events, social trends, and formulating highly questionable, murky and often incomprehensible conclusions from the data he accumulates. He enjoys aiding people who have stories to tell, but lack writing skills.

TL Blake is a world-traveler and adventure junkie. He says he likes to be where the action is, and tell it like it is. His travels have provided him with an array of experiences from which to draw while forming his often-radical views on women and relationships. His views are his own, but since his writing experience was limited, he sought the assistance and guidance of a more experienced writer.

TL Blake can be contacted via Forrest Nelson at http://forrestnelson.com, or at fnnewbie@gmail.com

Other books by Forrest Nelson:

Welcome to Fabulous Casino Surveillance

A look behind the cameras telling stories from thirty years in casino surveillance, some funny, some yucky, all entertaining. Find out what REALLY happened in The Eye in the Sky.

The Director's Report

The booklet the casinos hated seeing published. This work details how to turn losses on the casino tables into wins. Learn about card-counting, advantage play, how to keep from being cheated, and staying safe when visiting large resort casinos.